FOREWORD
BEST SELLING AUTHOR C

MW00974149

IF NOT NOW, WHEN?

An Introduction to Bravo Motivation

BY ATUL UCHIL

AWARD WINNING AUTHOR OF "REMEMBER THOU ART MORTAL"

outskirtspress
DENVER, COLORADO

Contents

Foreword

Over the last thirty plus years, I've read literally thousands of self-help, psychology, spirituality, and philosophy books because I've been infatuated with learning
about ways to obtain higher states of consciousness.
Self-actualization is a neatly packaged term for explaining what it must be like to arrive at an awareness
that is above the fear, stress, and anxiety that seems
to dominate the collective consciousness of the west.
Peace of mind is something we all crave but for some
reason most people look in all the wrong places to
find this elusive prize.

The book you are about to read is going to take you
on a wild ride, full of twists and turns, a crazy trip to
Thailand, a near-death experience, and stops along
the way to reflect on lessons learned about, not just
finding peace of mind, but finding meaning, purpose,
and an awareness of what's really important. The

exercises in this delightful book are simple, yet profound, and as I get older, and hopefully wiser in life,
I realize that the most useful information for moving
forward and becoming wiser is usually packaged in a
thin wrapper, and not weighted down with unnecessary packaging…just like this book.

Atul has created a book that seems more like a conversation with a good friend…a good friend who has
lived a very exciting life, and has learned some price-
less lessons along the way. The exercises in this book
and the wisdom attained from our guide's adventures
will give you a new perspective that can only help you
achieve greater clarity to see how to live your own life
now, with more joy, more purpose, and more peace of
mind, because IF NOT NOW, WHEN?

Derrick Sweet
Best Selling Author of "Get the Most Out of Life"

Acknowledgements

I dedicate this book to my wife **Patricia** for her uncon-
ditional support through the good and the not-so-good
times and for being my inspiration, my rock. I also
have to thank Patricia for giving me my kids **Lindsey**
(my daughter) and **Cory** (my son). Lindsey and Cory
bring me joy and meaning and, lest I forget, trials and
tribulations. However, they always light up my life.

My parents have been an inspiration my entire life.
They are the well from which I draw my strength. They
instilled in me discipline, honesty, integrity and perse-
verance. **Mom and Dad, I love you**.

Thank you Big Mike (papou) and Angie (yiaiya)
Kiriakou, you have always treated Patricia and me as
one of your own and made us feel welcome. Perry
Kiriakou, you have been and continue to be a big
brother to Patricia and me.

Phil Carrai has provided me with mentorship and guidance for more than half my career. Phil stood by me as a mentor and a friend through the years. Phil, you will always have my heartfelt gratitude and loyalty.

Major Jefferson (JD) Holden (USMC – Ret.), your friendship and loyalty knows no bounds. In addition to retiring honorably after serving our nation for 21 years, I remember your induction into the Cortland State University Athletic Hall of fame in 2005 for your accomplishments as a 6-time All-American and 1984 National Diving Champion. JD, my friend, I must also thank you for the 'Edamame stand.'

My friend Johnnie has requested that I not mention his last name. However, I am just going to say that if you seek reality on Boardwalk, you will surely find him. Sorry readers! This reference is something that only people who know Johnnie personally will understand.

Billy & Carolyn O'Dell, are wonderful people and truly warm friends. They live life with a zest and passion, which is a rare quality these days. They are also always willing to help others in any way they can.

Bill, Karen, Ray and Nancy Ashton, you have treated me as part of your family for the past two decades. You always accepted me for who I am through all the vicissitudes of my life. I feel proud to be associated with your family.

Thank you Kyle Holden for lending me your considerable photography skills in order to conceptualize and create the cover image for this book.

No book is ever completed without the help of many people whose friendship, advice and help are critical to the accomplishment of the project. To all of you that I have not explicitly mentioned here, I extend my gratitude for your help and my apologies for not having your name here.

SPECIAL THANKS: Derrick, I thank you for your willingness to write the foreword. I cannot say enough about Derrick Sweet. Derrick is the author of the best seller 'Get the Most Out of Life' and the founder of several corporations, including the Healthy, Wealthy and Wise Corporation.

However, this is just one aspect of Derrick. Most importantly, Derrick is truly a wonderful genuine human being and larger than life in many ways. He has dedicated himself to helping people and improving humanity in general.

The Planting of a Seed

I was conversing with my friend Johnnie, regarding the final edits for my book "Remember Thou Art Mortal."

Johnnie asked me if I had given thought to what I would write next.

"I have a title in mind." I replied.

Being the smart-aleck that he is, Johnnie quipped; "Are you going to tell me the title, or is it a big secret?"

"I think I will call it - I escaped, or something similar…" I trailed off.

"You escaped? What from?" Johnnie asked.

"I am not sure." I said, "I believe that I have escaped from many things in my life, the clutches of Corporate America for example or better yet, big city living?"

"I see you have given this a lot of deep thought." Johnnie snickered.

"Well, it's just an idea. I am still working on it. 'Remember Thou Art Mortal' has not been approved for publication yet." I said.

"Well then, let me know when you have given it thought and want to talk about it intelligently." Johnnie replied, while grinning from ear to ear like a Cheshire cat.

With this conversation, was planted a seed that germinated into the manuscript that you are reading today.

Before I proceed, let me tell you this. --- *I may use some words, language and expressions to explain various incidents as they happened. I am not normally in the habit of using strong (foul) language. However, some incidents will lose their flavor if I try to censor them. Therefore, I apologize in advance if I offend anyone's sensibilities. That is not my intent.* ---

I am willing to bet, you are probably wondering which escape is chronicled in this book. Well read on and find out. I am not going to spoil the surprise for you.

Several people have also told me that reading my books is just like having a conversation with me. I guess that makes sense. Because when I am in the process of writing a book, I write as if I am having a dialog with someone sitting in front of me.

Consequently, I invite you to join me in this dialog and hope that you enjoy the conversation.

One more caution: If you are looking for a well-structured book with information delivered in precise format, this may not be the best book for you. However, if you are looking for an abundance of relevant information interspersed with over almost a quarter century of real-life experiences, both good and bad, narrated with a lot of passion and caring, you will find this book stimulating and insightful.

I will let you be the judge.

The Seed Takes Root

A few months had passed after my conversation with Johnnie. I still did not know what I was going to write about or what I was going to call the book.

Picture this!

It is a pleasant October evening in Virginia Beach. Several friends are sitting around chatting and essentially relishing one of the advantages of living at the beach. Even though the calendar says, "summer is over," there are still many warm beach days in October and early November. Those of us that live at the beach especially look forward to enjoying these days prior to the onset of winter.

The daytime temperature on this particular day was in the mid-sixties. Billy and Carolyn were visiting from Barbados and we had all gathered at Perry's house overlooking the ocean.

Billy had just grilled up some steaks and chicken. Tracy had made some incredibly tasty veggie burgers, vegan meatloaf and vegetable kale soup for the vegetarians and vegans in the group and for those of us trying to adopt a primarily plant base diet. We had opened a bottle of wine and we were all sitting around the outdoor picnic table eating, relaxing and chatting.

"How is the business doing?" Billy asked me.

"Despite the recession, I am almost where I want to be. I think I have figured out how to thrive while working two or three days, averaging between twenty and twenty-five hours a week. I have not quite cracked the code on how to work less than twenty hours a week just yet. I am working on it though." I replied.

"We are also planning to downsize our house again." Patricia chimed in.

I must mention here that about eight years prior, we had downsized from three-thousand square feet to two-thousand three-hundred square feet. Now that we were empty nesters, we were looking to downsize again to a Condo between twelve hundred and fifteen hundred square feet.

"So when are you planning to downsize?" Billy asked.

"We are working on it." Patricia said. "We plan to get it done within the next year for sure."

"What's holding you back? What are you waiting for?" Billy asked.

"The timing is not quite right." I said. "I would like the market to stabilize some more."

To which Billy replied, "When the market stabilizes, there will be something else that will not be just right. The timing is never just right. You have to do the best you can within the current circumstances."

"You are right, Billy." I said.

Billy, Perry & Johnnie are extremely enterprising individuals. Moreover, each has achieved tremendous success while managing to maintain an easy-going attitude towards life and a healthy work life balance.

In many ways, I have always admired what each of them has been able to do. Not just in the business arena but in their overall attitude towards life.

Then our conversation turned to other matters and the topic of downsizing did not come up anymore that evening.

When Patricia and I came home from Perry's house, I tried to clear my mind and go to bed. However, sleep did not come easily that night. I tossed and turned while my mind kept mulling over the conversation that I had with Billy earlier in the evening.

This also brought to mind another conversation that I had with my friend JD Holden just one week earlier. JD and I were having dinner and got into what we term as one of our philosophical discussions. Of course, our wives roll their eyes at us when we get into these conversations. During this particular conversation, JD and I started discussing what it is we would do if/when we got out of the corporate world fully.

Suggestions covered the entire gamut from starting a fishing charter to developing a retirement community. I will not bore you with the details of the two-hour conversation. At some point during the evening, out of the blue, JD said, "what about an Edamame stand?"

"Edamame stand?" I said quizzically.

"Yes," JD replied, "Think about it, both of us really like helping people. We love to chat with people and listen to them. What's more, we both love the beach."

"What could be better than an Edamame stand on the beach? Fun in the sun while selling healthy snacks"

I had to admit that JD had a valid point. Yes, we both loved interacting with people and we loved the outdoors. However, the idea of standing out in the hot sun all day long through the summer did not seem very appealing to me.

Always one to mess with my head, JD said, "Of course,

the Edamame stand could just be a metaphor for whatever makes us happy and builds on our strengths."

Then the food arrived and our conversation turned to other topics, our kids, work, etc. My mind did not dwell on the Edamame stand at that particular time anymore.

Here I am a few months later, tossing and turning in an effort to fall asleep. I have two conversations running through my mind, the downsizing conversation with Billy and JD's Edamame stand.

While in that semi-daze somewhere between being asleep and awake, my mind starts decomposing JD's metaphorical Edamame stand. I start to wonder what my Edamame stand would look like. I wonder if or when I would get to enjoy my very own Edamame stand.

Suddenly a strange thought struck me. Why not start working on the Edamame stand now.

"If not now, when?" I said to myself.

In a flash, I jumped out of bed and dashed off into my office room.

"What happened now?" Patricia inquired.

"I have it. I know the title for the book." I replied. "I'm going to call it - If not now, when?"

All at once, I knew what I was going to write. I knew when I was going to write. The seed that was planted during that conversation with Johnnie had just taken root.

I was not going to write about escaping from anything after all. Once I jotted down the title, my mind was at rest and I knew I was ready to go to sleep. Therefore, I went back to bed.

As I was drifting off to sleep, my thoughts strayed to my life and the various experiences that had led me to this point.

I realized that I could define my life up to this point in four distinct phases.

- The early years in the UK
- The Corporate America years
- The race after the rat race
- The present

Before I tell you more about my life journey, let me take you on a slight detour and invite you to try something with me...

Believe

Success Redefined:

Let us ask ourselves the following question.

What is success? Better yet, ask yourself,

How do you define success?

I have posed this question to many people over the course of my career and the answers are varied. However, all of them seem to share a common theme. Most people define success as a destination.

I heard responses like:

"Success is achieving a desired outcome."

"Success is the accumulation of X dollars of wealth"

"Success is achieving the title of CXO or VP or "XYZ."

"Success is gaining experience, knowledge and expertise and being the foremost in your chosen field."

"Success is having power or fame." And so on…

I have often asked myself, "Is this really success? Is success just a destination?"

I have yet to meet a person who achieved a position or a title and said, "OK, I am a success, I have achieved the title I wanted so I can now stop what I am doing and/or resign."

It appears that achieving success at that juncture was just the culmination of a stage of life and became the foundation for the next dream, goal, ideal, etc.

Typically, a person, who decides to become a manager and achieves the desired position, does not stop when they achieve that promotion to manager. Even if they do not desire additional promotions, they still strive to perform well at their job. In effect, they have just redefined the criteria by which they measure their success.

Therefore, it stands to reason, that success is truly a journey and not a destination.

I guess, now that I have defined success on my terms, I should just stop and finish out my book. HA! HA! HA!

Not likely! I still have more to say.

Let us see how we can define success. Let us assume that you wake up one day and decide to be happy for the rest of that day. So now, your success criterion is happiness for one day. Let us further assume that you meet your criterion and spend the entire day happy.

Does this mean you are successful? Does this make you a success?

I believe it does. You have just achieved your goal and have successfully stayed happy for a whole day.

However, society has programmed us to define success in a purely materialistic manner.

I do not know how many of you remember the bumper sticker from the early nineties (I think) that said, **"He who dies with the most toys wins."**

I recently saw another bumper sticker. It said, **"He who dies with the most toys still dies."**

Either way, I feel that we are still setting ourselves up for failure if we continue to define success in a purely materialistic manner. Because, there is always a bigger house, bigger car, the next promotion, the next bigger company, the next fad, etc.

Let us do something different. Let us think of success differently. I invite you to join me in an exercise.

Come on, don't just sit there – try it with me.

Go out into your yard and move a stone. It does not have to be a large stone, just a small stone, a pebble or even a tiny grain of sand. Move it from one place to another. It does not have to be far. Just move it a little bit. Did you do something significant? What do you think?

If you are like I was when I did this initially, you are probably thinking, "what's the big deal, I moved a stone, or pebble, or a grain of sand"

Work with me on this experiment. Try to find success in the little things. You may not yet realize how much of an impact some little things have. My dad taught me this when I was young. Think back to when you moved dirt in a garden to plant something.

Or, when you simply threw a rock into a lake or pond.

Or, when you moved a small grain of sand.

Now think of what you have accomplished by performing any of these actions. Think…

Did you get it yet? No?

Think harder…

Still no?

All right, let me tell you. By moving even the tiniest grain of sand, you have in effect changed the face of the earth.

If it seems incomprehensible, let me try to clarify the concept, as I understand.

What is that stone, pebble or tiny grain of sand? It is a collection of atoms, molecules, protons, neutrons, electrons, etc. In other words, it is a mass of matter. I believe, we can all agree on this part.

Now let us extrapolate. Several tiny masses of matter, come together to make up a larger mass of matter. Everything around us and ultimately, even the earth is made up of a collection of masses of matter. Therefore, by moving that tiny grain of sand, you have changed the face of the earth.

I know that some of you are still unconvinced. Some of you agree with me, maybe begrudgingly.

Then, there are those of you that are awestruck. Yes! You got it. Your eyes are open to possibilities.

I ask you to start looking at things in a different way. I further ask you to try to see the greatness in little things.

Once you do, you will realize how powerful you really are. I mean, what can be more powerful than having the ability to change the face of the earth?

Do you feel it?

Let me repeat myself. Do you really feel it?

YOU ARE POWERFUL.

Don't just read it. Say it.

Repeat after me. "I AM POWERFUL."

"I HAVE THE ABILITY TO CHANGE THE FACE OF THE EARTH."

No! No! No! Not half-heartedly.

Say it as if you believe it and mean it.

Believe in what you are saying before you say it again.

Don't just whisper it or speak it. Shout it out. Let us try this again. Loudly now. As loud as you can.

"I AM POWERFUL."

"I HAVE THE ABILITY TO CHANGE THE FACE OF THE EARTH."

How does this make you feel?

Do you feel like some energy just coursed through your veins?

Well did it?

Do you feel like you are filled with anticipation about what you can do next?

In my opinion, success is about the person you are, and the person you are becoming. It is about fulfilling your potential and achieving your dreams.

Your individual success is whatever brings you a life of joy and fills you with joyous anticipation. Once you start to believe, you will see wonder in the tiniest of things. You will start anticipating every moment and life will become an adventure.

The exercise that we performed is an exercise in Belief.

This was just the first amongst several exercises that we are going to try together as we progress through this book.

If you take away one word from this chapter, it should be

BELIEVE.

Now that you **BELIEVE**, let me take you back to my journey.

I had originally intended to end the chapter at this juncture. However, my friend Derrick told me that I needed to elaborate a little bit more on the concept of BELIEVE. He advised me to give you one more example.

Therefore, here goes. If you are still skeptical about the concept of BELIEVE, please try this with me.

Note: If you have already accepted the concept of BELIEVE, you may choose to move on to the next chapter.

If you are still with me, please make a list of all the things you believe in that are outside your control: For example:

- I believe that the sun will rise tomorrow.
- I believe that there will be enough oxygen in the air for me to breathe and live.
- I believe that I can find my way from my house to my office.
- I believe that the spring will follow the winter.
- I believe that my car will start when I turn the keys and that it will move when I put it in gear.
- And so on…

In each of these cases, you believe that something that is completely outside your control will happen.

Ask yourself this. "Why then do I not believe in my own abilities?"

Repeat after me.

"My abilities are within my control."

"I believe I can accomplish anything into which I put my effort."

One more time.

"My abilities are within my control."

"I believe I can accomplish anything into which I put my effort."

And, once more.

"My abilities are within my control."

"I believe I can accomplish anything into which I put my effort."

And, once last time.

"My abilities are within my control."

"I believe I can accomplish anything into which I put my effort."

Do you feel a tiny bit of self-assurance? Do you believe you can achieve some tasks, however small?

Excellent!

You are now ready to move on.

The Early Years in the UK

I was born in early September. Yep, I am a Virgo. I lived in London for most of the early years of my life. To be precise, I lived in a place called Romford in Essex County.

Romford is a sleepy little town. At least it used to be when I was young. It is located roughly about thirty minutes train ride by British Rail from the Liverpool Street Station on the Sheffield line. I bet you are wondering why I am imposing this geography lesson on you. It is because I want to emphasize the great difference in the pace of life that even a small distance of thirty miles creates, especially in Europe. To begin with, most big cities in Europe appear laidback when compared to most of the big cities in the US like Chicago, New York and DC. Try to imagine how laid back the small rustic towns appear in comparison.

Romford is such a town, where families live in the same house for generations and everybody knows everyone else. This also means that everything that goes on in the town is everyone else's business. This is most definitely not a good scenario for a rambunctious and rowdy teenager. Believe me when I say that news traveled fast. Moreover, it seemed to travel even faster when I was involved. At least that is how I felt.

I vividly remember getting into my first fistfight. I won, or so I thought until I got home and my dad was waiting for me on the front porch (we called it a veranda), demanding to know why I was behaving like a street hooligan. Well, saying I got a reaming that night would be an understatement.

The cops (Bobbies) knew us all by sight and name. In addition, most of them went to the local pub with our parents. Therefore, it was a double whammy, if they caught you doing something that you should not have been doing. They would not arrest you. Instead, they would put you in the back of their vehicle and drive you to your home. As a result, your parents would be doubly mad. Not only had you done something stupid, but also the whole neighborhood had seen you brought home in the paddy wagon. I would have preferred that they took me to jail.

The guiding light in my childhood was my paternal grandma Mae. She was a small and tough Scottish woman who brought me up with stern discipline. I provided the stern and she provided the discipline. Just kidding! Actually, she instilled in me the old school values of honesty, integrity, hard work and dedication to duty.

She would sit me by her side every evening and tell me stories about how her parents moved from Scotland to England and how they settled in Romford. She also told me many Scottish fables and stories of Scottish heroes. These included stories of Mary Queen of the Scottish Isles, King Robert the Bruce and much more.

Then every night just before it was time to go to bed, she made me say aloud a prayer that she had taught me.

My grandma passed on when I was seven. However, her words of prayer still resound in my head even to-day. "I will not do anything during the course of a day that will make me afraid to meet my maker should he come calling that night." She told me, if I lived life by the words in this prayer, they would be my bible and my church.

Anyway, I digress. I was talking about the pace of life in Romford. People worked four and a half days a week. It seemed that way since most of them were at the pub by three pm on Friday. Small town UK pubs are much more a social gathering place and much less a 'for drinking' place. Moreover, in small towns in the UK, it is the older crowd that usually frequents the pubs as opposed to the much younger crowd in large cities.

People typically worked from nine to five, eight to four, or some combination of eight-hour days. Almost everyone gets four weeks of vacation a year at a minimum. The lucky ones get five or six weeks. Vacation in the UK is mandatory unlike the US. You cannot work it out or cash it out. By law, you had to take your vacation. Consequently, if December came around and you had not used up all of your four weeks of vacation, your company asked you to go home and come back in the New Year (paid of course).

As my memory serves me, no one in Romford was filthy rich as far back as I can remember. However, almost everyone gave the appearance of being comfortably well off. I grew up seeing these things as a way of life. I took for granted that this was the quality of life for everyone else in the world.

Since Paris and Rome were within easy access, I learned about art at an early age. My father and I made several trips to museums. Dad was always patient in his response and explanations to my endless questions. Consequently, I gained a deep appreciation for the art and architecture of the great masters of the renaissance early in my life.

On one of our vacations, my dad took us to Paris where we visited the Louvre and Musée Rodin. There

I fell in love with the works of Augusté Rodin. The 'Idole Eternale' and 'The Kiss' evoked forbidden mental images of secret passions and awe at the ability of Rodin to capture thought into sculpture.

A trip to Rome and the Galleria Borghese made me fall in love with the works of Antonio Canova. Sculptures of the reclining 'Paolina Borghese' sister to Napoleon Bonaparte, and the forgiven 'Cupid and Psyche' were simply divine. I spent hours just staring at the detail in these sculptures. Canova carved the Cupid and Psyche in infinitesimal detail right down to the fingernails.

Soon after this, my dad introduced me to books on art. A completely new world opened up to me. No longer would I have to sate my curiosity by reading the one measly paragraph that the museum displayed next to a painting or sculpture. I was now able to understand the history of the artist and the stories behind their creations.

I collected all the books on art I could find and afford on my allowance. I spent hours on end reading about the story behind each sculpture or painting. The architecture of Gianlorenzo Bernini, the paintings of Sandro Boticelli, the sheer genius of Michelangelo; I was enamored with all of this and more.

Music had not escaped my attention either. I learned to feel (I specifically mean 'feel' not 'hear') the haunting melodies of Edith Piaf, Gilbert Becaud, Yves

Montand, Charles Trenet and last but not the least Charles Aznavour. I dare not forget to mention my Dad's favorite Cliff Richards. These were my nightly lullabies for many years.

I believed then that life was meant truly to be like this, slow, serene, filled with beauty and love.

I also excelled in school. I am a fastidious type 'A' personality and a fast learner. Moreover, I had little or no distractions at school. I attended Doveton Corrie Protestant Boys' Missionary School. The key word here is Boys' school. As in no girls. Moreover, all of us wore the same uniforms right down to our shoes.

I loved all challenges and any competition. It goes without saying, that I was a troublemaker. I would be done with my class-work faster than most other kids and then disrupt the class. As a solution, teachers started giving me additional work to keep me occupied. Much to their dismay, I began finishing the additional work faster too and still had enough time on my hands to cause trouble.

After one of many parent teacher conferences, my parents and the school jointly decided that fourth grade by itself was not enough of a challenge for me. Their plan was that while I was still in fourth grade, the teachers would give me both fourth and fifth grade work. This plan went into effect almost immediately, courtesy of the absence of red tape at private schools.

Moreover, my mom was also a schoolteacher for ninth and tenth grade math. She volunteered to tutor me on any fifth grade subjects that I could not figure out for myself. Therefore, I received the opportunity to finish the fourth and fifth grade course work while I was still in fourth grade.

Consequently, I skipped a grade in school and went directly from fourth grade to sixth grade. As a result, I finished high school a full year earlier than my peer age group. This afforded me the time to go on a year-long backpacking tour of the world. At that time, I naively thought that I could see all the art there was to see, experience different cultures, feel different music and get lost in all the beauty that the world had to offer.

Although, I visited several countries, I did not quite see the entire world as I had planned. I had fun most of the time. Not surprisingly, I also had a few misadventures. One fiasco in particular stands out and is worth mentioning here. This happened when I was in Bangkok. Hmmmmm! How can I best describe what happened to me in Bangkok. There is no way around it. I managed to get myself arrested.

You probably want to hear the whole story, do you not? Well, I managed to get myself arrested for soliciting and assaulting a male prostitute.

I know it sounds shocking. However, in reality, it is

not as bad as it sounds. Now let me tell you what really happened. After a long flight, I landed at Don Muang International Airport. It was hot and humid. Almost like Miami in July.

I had made a reservation, through my dad's travel agent, at the Baiyoke Suite Hotel, Bangkok in the Pratunam district. It was a very reasonably priced hotel by any standards. The nightly room rate was eight hundred and fifty Bhat including all taxes, which translates to approximately twenty-two US dollars.

Bangkok is capital of Thailand and some consider it one of most dynamic cities in Asia. It is a city bustling with people. This steamy tropical city offers surprises at every turn. Modern skyscrapers coexist with traditional temples. You can find upscale shopping malls blocks away from local street markets. Bangkok has a thriving nightlife and I am going to leave that part to everyone's imagination.

Anyway, back to my situation. I was tired and jet lagged. The intense heat and humidity was not helping my situation either. I managed to find my hotel, check in and then I crashed from sheer exhaustion. I slept through the night and most of the next morning until I woke at about eleven am local time feeling refreshed. I was determined not to waste my day so I showered and headed to the lobby. I secured a map of the local area in the hotel lobby. After carefully marking the location of the hotel on the map, I set off on foot to explore this beautiful city.

I must have wandered through the city for several hours on foot before I realized that I was famished and a little light headed from hunger. I needed food fast. Not knowing the area, I followed my nose until I came across what looked like a restaurant-bar. Those of you that have visited Bangkok, know exactly what I mean by followed my nose. For the rest of you, any market is Bangkok usually has street food vendors and your olfactory senses are under a constant assault the various smells. Anyway back to the restaurant-bar, it certainly smelled like palatable food. Therefore, I went in.

Once inside, I realized that it was more a bar than a restaurant. Through the dim lighting, I made out a regular bar with a bartender behind it. They also had several booths with tables that were shaped like a "C". It looked like a seat yourself kind of place. Therefore, I plopped myself down in one of those booths.

The menus were already on the table and they were not in English. Surprise, they were printed in the local language, which to me might as well have been hieroglyphics. I am an adventurous eater in general. At that point, I was so famished; I would have eaten almost anything. I closed my eyes and placed my finger on the menu.

When the waiter came by to take my order, I pointed to the menu item that I had picked. He said "Bhat" and rubbed his forefinger and thumb together. I was a little surprised because I had never eaten at a restaurant that asked for money up front. I gave him twenty Bhat (about fifty cents) and he did not give me back any change.

A few moments later, while I was waiting for my food, a man came by and sat down beside me. I was surprised, but not knowing the local customs, I nodded politely and smiled. He asked something in broken English.

The words he used sounded like, "yo foreeen; yo toureeest."

I assumed he meant, "Are you foreign; are you a tourist?" Therefore, I nodded my head in the affirmative and said yes.

He then began a talking to me in Thai with a few English words thrown in. I heard the words 'Foreign', 'Tourist' and 'Bhat' mentioned several times. I assumed that he was asking me for a handout. I told him that I did not believe in giving monetary handouts but I would gladly buy him a meal.

I was certain that he did not understand what I had just said. So I handed him the menu and pointed to him and then to the menu and made an eating gesture.

He seemed delighted, yelled out loudly for the waiter, and ordered something off the menu. I once again gave the waiter twenty Bhat. When the waiter started to turn away just as he did before, the man started talking to the waiter in a very animated manner. This time the waiter laid ten Bhat back on the table. The man turned to me and smiled all proud of himself. I really did not care, to me was only twenty-five cents.

When the waiter delivered the food, I was pleased. It was piping hot and it smelled delicious. Thankfully, the dish that I had ordered looked and tasted like some form of curry chicken. I just dug right in and began to eat.

My table companion continued our one-sided conversation. He kept talking incessantly and I kept smiling politely and nodding occasionally. I assumed that he was thanking me for the meal. Then he did something that caught me completely by surprise. While conversing, he reached over and started rubbing my crotch.

I was so surprised that I reacted by reflex before thinking and swung out my fist. My fist caught him flush in the mouth and busted his lip open. He screamed loudly. The next thing I remember is that there were several people pinning me to the floor. It was futile to struggle, as there were too many. A few moments later, two police officers came in. They cuffed me, put me in the back of their vehicle and carted me off to the police station.

I was a little perturbed but not too terribly concerned. I thought that as soon as I was able to explain the circumstances to someone in authority, they would let me go with an apology. When we got to the police station, I was marched to a room.

The two police officers walked me in, took my handcuffs off and locked the door behind them. The room was completely bare, with one rickety old wooden chair and bars on the door. I assumed that someone would come and talk to me soon. I looked at my wristwatch and noticed that it was about five pm local time.

Time moves very slowly when you have nothing to do. Every minute seems long and tedious. Time dragged on. At one point, I thought I had been there for hours and when I looked at my watch, it was only forty minutes. I had not started to panic yet. However, I was getting more nervous with every passing minute. I began pacing. When I got tired of pacing, I sat down. I was too restless to sit down for long, so I began pacing again.

I continued this alternate pacing and sitting routine for about two hours. Then something inside me snapped. I stuck my face up to the bars on the door and yelled.

"I am a British citizen. Someone needs to call the British embassy."

The only response I got back was a series of angry shhhhh's and what I assume were several expletives in the local language. Thankfully, I did not understand the words.

It was then that I began to panic. No one knew exactly where I was, not even my parents. What if they never let me get out of here? Who would find me? These and many other weird thoughts kept running through my head and driving me crazy.

Finally, a little after eleven pm I heard a key in the lock. Mind you, I had been in that cell for over six hours. I was physically and mentally exhausted, hungry and afraid. A police officer dressed all in white uniform opened the door and beckoned me to follow him. He looked more like a navy officer that a police officer. I followed him to what I presume was his office where he stated in a very businesslike manner "I am superintendent of police Bramhatsu," (fictitious name) and did not offer to shake my hand. He then pointed to the chair in front of his desk, so I sat down.

I thought he was just being curt and formal, until he spoke his next words.

"We hate people like you coming to our country," he said.

I was completely taken aback by his statement.

I had heard that there was a certain level of dislike

towards westerners in several parts of the world. However, Bangkok was a popular tourist destination and I was certain that they got their fair share of tourists every year.

"So you hate Caucasians," I asked perplexed.

His reply only added to my confusion. "Not Caucasians, just people like you."

"You mean you hate the British," I asked incredulously.

"Do not hate the British, just your type of people. We would rather not have you here in our country."

"I see it now," I said. "You hate people of mixed races."

"Not your race, just you." He responded.

By this time, I was thoroughly confused. I had absolutely no idea why he hated me. Therefore, in the calmest tone of voice that I could muster under the circumstances, I said, "You obviously don't like me for some reason that is beyond my control and comprehension. But that's OK."

I continued, "You need to call the British Embassy because I am a British citizen."

"The guy that I hit touched my privates. Where I come from we do not put up with stunts like that."

He looked at me as if he was surprised at my words and then said. "Let me ask you sir, are you or are you not a homosexual."

"No, I am not gay," I said, "Why do you think I punched the guy when he touched my privates?"

He then asked, "Why did you go there in the first place?"

I explained about wandering around the city sightseeing, feeling the pangs of hunger and going in there to eat.

He responded in a much nicer tone of voice, "Do you know what that place is?"

"I think, I know now," I said, "I guess it is a gay bar."

"No, not a gay bar," he said. "That bar is a front for male prostitution and the person you assaulted is a convicted male prostitute."

"So now that I have explained the situation can I leave?" I asked.

He looked at me and said; "No sir, you have just explained the solicitation charge."

"What else is there?" I asked.

"Assault," he said, "After all you hit the man and we do have laws in this country."

"However, this can be resolved with a small fine," he continued. "Is fifty dollars American too much?"

"No problem," I said. "But I do not have it on me. I have Traveler's Checks in my hotel room."

"What hotel?" he asked.

"The Baiyoke Suite Hotel," I replied.

He told me that he was going to escort me to my hotel to collect the fine. I began to revise my opinion of the man rather rapidly. He was only doing his job before, I said to myself. When we got to the hotel, he escorted me to my room. I reached into the hidden lining in my suitcase and got out a Traveler's Check for fifty dollars.

"Could you please sign it and counter sign it, sir," he said.

"But if I do that anyone can cash it," I commented as I signed.

"I know," he replied.

Then he picked up the Traveler's Check, folded it neatly, put it in the pocket of his tunic, shook my hand and said, "Sir, I hope you enjoy your stay in Bangkok."

With these words, he abruptly turned and left the room.

The moment the door to the room swung shut, I used my calling card and called home. As soon as my father answered, the first words out of my mouth were; "Dad, guess what I did today? I bribed a police officer."

I visited many countries. I had several adventures but that is a subject best left for another time.

I concluded my yearlong journey on the Atlantic coast of the US, where I fell in love with the glamour and extravagance of New York and the hustle and bustle of Washington, DC. These cities seemed to pulse with energy.

Life in the US seemed very different when compared to life in Europe. The impact that these cities had on my young mind was very profound. Try as I might, I could not shake it. I resolved to continue my education in the United States of America. I was still planning to go back to merry old Romford after I had completed my education, mind you. At least that is what I believed at the time.

Having made up my mind, I spent the final days of my vacation in the US gathering information on schools and admission processes and other such necessary details.

When I went back home, I was prepared. I had all the information that I needed to take the SAT (Scholastic Aptitude Test) and the TOEFL (Test of English as

Foreign Language). Apparently, some US Universities do not recognize the UK as an English speaking country. I was very determined to secure admission to an American University.

Little did I know then I was starting down a path that would eventually culminate in an all-consuming addiction!

I promised you several exercises and I am a person who keeps his word. So, before I tell you more about my journey, let me invite you to the next exercise...

Recognize

Before you start reading, you are going to need a pen or pencil and a pad of paper for this exercise. Please get these items before you start the exercise.

Now, close your eyes and imagine this. Somehow, you have all the money you need so that you do not have to work a single day for the rest of your life. It is not important how you got the money. Just picture that you have the money and it is safe in the bank.

Are you there in your mind? Do you feel the money sitting in the bank account waiting for you? Are you basking in the comforting thought that you do not have to work anymore to pay the bills?

Great!

Now, let me ask you a question. "What type of work would you want to do?"

I mean. "What do you really want to do?"

"What is that dream activity that you would want to do forever, regardless of whether you were paid for it or not?"

"What is it that you would enjoy so much that you would leave the house to do it even when you have all the money you will even need for the rest of your life?"

"What is your hidden passion, your dream?"

I hope you are taking this seriously. If not, I request you to take this exercise seriously. Because, it creates the foundation for the exercises that will follow.

Please close your eyes and give some thought to this dream. It does not necessarily have to be a job. It could be some activity, volunteering, or living the island life.

Why am I giving you answers? I cannot read your mind and it is your dream after all. So, I'll shut up for the moment and give you time to think.

If you have this in mind, please write it down. Are you done? Have you written it down?

Excellent!

Now, let me ask you another question. What is keeping you from following this dream today?

Please do not just say money or bills. Give this some serious thought.

Now in a most unauthorlike manner, and after just having made up the word "unauthorlike," I am actually going to ask you to put down the book and take some time to yourself.

Hold on. Not just yet...

Please bookmark this page. Spend a few hours thinking about what it is that is keeping you from pursuing your dream today. Write down everything you can think about on a sheet of paper.

I am certain that money and bills are on the list. Create the rest of your list and I will see you in a few hours...

Ah! You are back. At least, I hope it is you. Well then, what does you list look like?

I have shared this exercise with every single one of my coaching clients. In addition to money and bills, I have found that it may include skills, certifications, training, not knowing how to get started, etc.

We will talk a little more about this in a later chapter. For now, I want you to organize your thoughts in the following format.

Please create a table that looks like the one below on a fresh sheet of paper.

My Dream life is _____		
The things I RECOGNIZE that keep me from pursuing my dream life are: - Item 1 - Item 2 - Item 3 - Item 4 - - - -		

Excellent!

Now, let me ask you another question. What skills, knowledge and capabilities do you possess?

Please bookmark this page. Spend a few hours thinking about your skills and capabilities. Write down everything you can think about on a sheet of paper.

I am certain that a few things will pop up very quickly,

like your education or skills that you have learned at work. However, give it some deep thought. Here is an example of what I personally did. When I was leaving corporate America, I decided to make a list of my skills.

After going through education and direct work skills, and thinking deeper, I realized that I had learned to negotiate and mediate because of working with employee issues. I also realized that I had acquired skills of mentoring, coaching, accounting, budgeting, and believe it or not HTML coding.

No! I am not a programmer. I was never a programmer. I will never be a programmer. However, I had managed a project that involved some detailed web design. We ran into problems and I had to help the client, figure out exactly how to get what they wanted in their website, while staying within the technical limitations that my engineers were facing. This statement is a euphemism for – "I was acting as a translator between the demanding client and my whiny engineers."

I inadvertently picked up basic HTML coding practices. I never realized that I had acquired this skill. Then one day, my friend Perry was talking to me about his company website and I started telling him what he needed to ask of his programmers. Perry asked me, "So when did you learn HTML programming."

To which I replied, "Brother, you know fully well that I do not understand programming."

"You surely could have fooled me." Perry responded.

Then the realization hit me and I told Perry about how I may have picked up a little because of the project I mentioned earlier.

Therefore, I urge you to please give this some serious thought and take some time to yourself. Create your list and I will see you in a few hours...

I hope you are back and have a list that looks something like this.

I have learned many things in my life and career. Here is a list of the things I have learned.

The skills and capabilities that I RECOGNIZE I have are:

- Skill 1
- Skill 2
- Skill 3
- Skill 4
-

-

-

Excellent!

Keep this list with you. We will use it later in the book.

As a result of this exercise, you have RECOGNIZED

your true passion. You have also RECOGNIZED what you think is keeping you from pursuing your passion. Moreover, you have RECOGNIZED your strengths, skills and abilities.

Now that you **RECOGNIZE**, let me take you back to my journey.

My First Taste of Corporate America

When I got back to Romford after my yearlong vacation, I studied hard and appeared for the SAT and the TOEFL. I fared very well at both the SAT and TOEFL. Immediately after getting my results, I began the arduous task of selecting and applying to universities. How does someone who has limited knowledge of the US education system choose the right university? I considered flipping a coin. No way! That would be too easy and more appropriately too risky!

I decided instead to read every piece of literature I could find on the universities that seemed interesting to me. I picked my initial list of universities randomly from a whole pile of brochures that I had acquired. I guess I should have flipped that coin after all. I read multitudes of similar sounding brochures for weeks. They all talked about the academic qualifications, student life, and excellent faculty. Suddenly, one statement piqued my interest.

"We are the cultural melting pot of the United States," it said. "We house students from over eighty nationalities."

This was in the information booklet sent to me by Cleveland State University.

I had found it. This was where I wanted to study. I was already going to have the option and ability to learn about the American culture by virtue of being in America. However, as an added bonus I would get to meet people from so many different nationalities and so many different cultures. On second thought, I really should have just flipped the coin.

I applied to Cleveland State University and several others as backups, just in case. Then the waiting period began in earnest. It was nerve wracking to say the least. I had never cared much about whether the mail carrier delivered the mail or not or about what time he came to deliver the mail. However, from the day I sent in my applications, I waited for the mail every single day, with anxious anticipation.

I found out from my mom that the mail carrier usually delivered the mail around one pm. I would look out the window at least twenty times from about twelve fifty pm until I saw the mail carrier heading towards our mailbox. I usually followed this up with a mad dash down the cobblestone path to get to the mail as soon as the mail carrier placed it in our mailbox. I kept up this routine for almost four weeks. I am sure I drove my mom crazy. However, despite what she may have thought, she appeared very understanding she did not comment on my bizarre behavior.

Finally, the letter I that was waiting for arrived. I remember clearly, it was a Wednesday. The return address said the words Cleveland State University and Official Business. It was a plain white size ten envelop.

My heart was beating like a trip hammer. Surely, if they had accepted me, they would send me something more substantial. What if they did not accept me? What if I did not fill out the application correctly? What if my high school did not send the transcripts to the Universities that they were supposed to?

"Just open it Atul," my mom's voice echoed, pragmatic as usual.

"You are not going to find out what is inside by staring at that envelop," she added for good measure.

"OK! Help me God! This is all I will ever ask from you." I prayed silently as I tore the envelop open. All right, read Atul read…

"Dear Mr. Uchil; we are pleased to extend you an

offer of admission..." Yippeeeeee. I made it, I was in, all my dreams were about to come true.

A few days of jubilation and celebration were followed by weeks of preparation for my journey to America. I was the toast of the pub that Friday evening, as my parents bought everyone a round of drinks to commemorate my accomplishment.

I wanted to pack everything I possessed. However, the weight restrictions enforced by the airlines severely limited what I could take. I had to make many tough decisions. I was undertaking a major relocation. I had to let go of the many treasures (junk actually) that I had collected during my childhood.

The cheapest ticket that I could find was through Continental Airlines. The itinerary had me coming into Newark, New Jersey as my port of entry into the US and then connecting to a puddle jumper headed for Cleveland, Ohio. I planned everything down to the finest detail. All the proverbial T's were crossed and I's were dotted. The only thing that I could do now was to wait impatiently for my departure day to arrive.

When the day finally arrived, I experienced eager anticipation intermingled with a twinge of sadness. It was the third of September, a few days shy of my 18th birthday. My mom and dad took me to Heathrow airport. My mom sobbed the entire way. Her little baby had grown up and was leaving home. After several hugs, many kisses on both cheeks and more tears, I walked through customs and began my journey.

A feeling of trepidation slowly swamped my eager anticipation. I knew deep down that many new adventures awaited me in America. Nevertheless, I was also leaving everything I knew behind me.

Things went off without a hitch at Heathrow airport. I got through departure customs, checked in and waited in the international passengers' lounge for my flight. The flight was uneventful also, albeit a little longer than scheduled due to the strong headwinds caused by the jet stream.

When I landed, I experienced joyous anticipation once again. I had arrived in the land of opportunity. I got through immigration and customs with no problems. I remember the officer at immigration stamping my passport and saying, "you're all set." This was my first new American phrase. I thought it was adorable. "you're all set."

It is true that people speak English in the US and in the UK. However, the colloquialisms could not be more different. Hence my intrigue with such a simple phrase.

I went to the big departure screen to find gate information for my Cleveland flight. It was then that everything began to go wrong. Much to my dismay, I found out that my connecting flight was cancelled. Still determined not to let anything dampen my spirits, I made my way to the Continental airlines customer service counter and waited in line.

When it was my turn, the ticketing agent was very helpful. She informed me that since the flight was cancelled due to mechanical reasons, I was automatically booked on the next flight. Things were looking up again. All I had to do was wait another four hours for the next flight. No problem, I thought, I can hang around Newark airport for a few hours and people-watch. Watching how people act and interact has always fascinated me. Therefore, the four hours passed quickly.

I had only one nagging worry in the back of my mind. The University had informed me in their correspondence that they usually sent someone to meet new international students at the airport. This person would be my peer student advisor who would guide me through the registration process and familiarize me with the University.

I hoped that the peer student advisor would be resourceful enough to get information about the flight cancellation and my being bumped to the next flight. I hoped he or she would wait for me at Cleveland airport or designate an alternate person to meet me. I was reasonably certain that at the very least they would leave a message with some directions on how I could get from the airport to the university and what I should do when I get there. I have never been so completely wrong in my life.

When I finally took the next flight from Newark and landed at Cleveland Hopkins International airport, it was a little past midnight. I went to the baggage carousel and waited for my luggage. The carousel kept turning and suitcases kept popping out. People picked up their respective luggage and went their respective ways. I waited patiently but I could not see my suitcases anywhere. When the flow of luggage dwindled, I began to get worried that my suitcases were misplaced. Therefore, I went to the Continental airlines lost luggage counter.

The person at the counter looked at the luggage stubs attached to my boarding card jacket and began pecking at his computer keyboard. After a few moments he said, "Good news sir, we have located your luggage."

"Great" I said, "where can I pick them up?"

"That's the problem you see, your bags were put on the wrong plane and went to Cincinnati," he answered.

"So what do I do now?" was my rather unhappy query.

"We will get your bags to you first thing tomorrow morning; just leave us a delivery address." He said reassuringly.

I was not going to take any chances. I found out what time they expected the bags to arrive in the morning. Then I told him that I would prefer coming back in the morning to collect my bags in person. He gave me a small receipt and told me to hang on to it.

I got out of the airport and went to the arriving passenger pickup area. I expected to see the peer student advisor, as promised by the University, holding a placard with my name on it. Nope, no such luck. I found out later, that when the peer student advisor assigned to me learned my flight was cancelled, he went back to the University and informed them that he had waited until the appointed time and that I had not arrived on my scheduled flight. So much for dedication to duty!

Having nowhere to go, and being unfamiliar with the city, I looked up the motels advertised at the airport. I found one close to the airport and walked the one-mile distance to that motel. Almost everyone told me later, that it was very foolish of me to walk, in that part of Cleveland alone, late at night.

I gave the motel desk clerk sixty-two dollars in Travelers Checks and settled in for the night. I must have been completely exhausted because the next thing I remember was waking up at nine am.

I showered, put on the same clothes in which I had traveled and headed back to the airport. True to their word, my luggage was at the Continental airlines luggage counter. I picked up my luggage and caught a cab for the University.

Cleveland State University does not have a walled off campus like many other Universities. It is located on Euclid Avenue (a major road) in downtown Cleveland and occupies several buildings between East Eighteenth and East Twenty-Sixth Streets.

The cabbie dropped me off at the intersection of East Twenty-Fourth Street and Euclid Avenue. There I stood in the middle of downtown Cleveland with three pieces of luggage and not quite sure where I was supposed to go. A student walked by and asked me if I needed help. At least, I assumed she was a student because of the armful of books that she was carrying. "I need to register," I said, "But first I would like to find a place to park my belongings."

"Where are you staying?" she asked. When she learned that I was staying at the dorms, she pointed to the building directly across the street and said, "Those are the dorms."

I made my way to the dorms. I caught a big break. The people at the front desk in the dorms were expecting me. After cross-referencing my passport to the names of international students on their list, they helped my get to my room. They also gave me my student ID number. Armed with my student ID number, a map of the University campus, a fresh change of clothes and a shave, I went in search of student registration.

I found the student registration room with some difficulty. To my delight, they had all the relevant information on my admission and my scholarship. I forgot to mention earlier, a significant part of my trepidation and anxiety in London waiting for the mail carrier was because I had applied for a scholarship. Needless to say, I got the scholarship.

I looked through the course curriculum for the fall quarter and selected the courses that I thought made most sense for a budding electrical engineer. It took all of fifteen minutes for me to complete the registration formalities for the quarter.

Realizing that the rumblings I heard were not thunder but actually my stomach, I asked the person at the registration counter where I could go to get some food. I received more good news. I learned that when my scholarship mentioned tuition, room and board, it meant that I was entitled to two meals a day at the cafeteria located in the University dorms. All I needed to access my meal privileges was my student ID card.

Off I went, with copies of my registration, my passport and every other piece of paper that I had accumulated to acquire my student ID card. No problems there either, except the picture was not a very good one. I looked like I had not slept in days. I wonder why. HA HA HA.

After a hearty lunch of cafeteria food, I began to wander around the campus just to familiarize myself. I came across a bulletin board full of help wanted ads.

I must mention here that the official start of the quarter was one week away. The university had recommended that first-time international students arrive a week to ten days before the official start of the quarter. They advised us to utilize this week to familiarize ourselves with the layout of the campus and its services.

Back to the bulletin board and the help wanted ads. I was intrigued and spent a few moments reading them more out of curiosity and less out of necessity. I noticed that most jobs promised minimum wage. The scholarship covered almost all my basic needs and I had a few thousand dollars saved up. Therefore, I was not too terribly worried about money.

However, one ad jumped out at me. The dorms needed a night shift student access monitor for the midnight to eight am shift on Mondays, Wednesdays and Fridays. The job paid five dollars an hour. Minimum wage was three dollars and eighty-five cents per hour at the time. The position paid extra money above minimum wage because most students did not want to work the midnight shift. The contact person listed on the ad was the resident dorm director. I had just met her that morning and she seemed like a very nice person.

I made my way back to the dorms, ad in hand and looked her up. I was not sure what to expect in the interview. She actually seemed delighted to hear that someone wanted the job. She asked me why I was interested in the job. My reply was prompt and earnest. I told her about the 'cultural melting pot' thing and my desire to meet new people and learn about the American culture and any other cultures that I could learn.

"What better way to meet people, other than as the access monitor?" I said.

"I will see and talk with many more people than I would by just being a regular student." I continued.

She did not seem to care one way or the other about my sincere statement or my desire to meet people. I guess her question was just to check a box on the interview sheet she had in front of her.

Having secured the job, I wandered around the campus for another hour or so. I wanted to do more and explore the rest of the campus. However, even though the spirit was willing, the body was not cooperating. Jetlag was catching up with me big time. I decided to give my tired body some rest. I found my way back to my dorm room and crawled into bed.

I awakened approximately two hours later to the sound of a series of knocks on my dorm room door. I hastily donned my jeans and opened the door, jeans half zipped up and no shirt. I saw a man in tie and several wide-eyed students behind him.

"What's all the fuss about?" I enquired.

"Are you Aye toll?" He asked.

"Yes, and it's A-Tool, like a hammer or screwdriver." I responded.

He introduced himself as Dr. Burke the dean of international admissions.

Having received the report from the peer advisor of my not arriving, the dean of international admissions had contacted the airline and found that I had indeed arrived in Cleveland. Now he was worried and a little panicked because he thought he had a missing international student on his hands. While accompanying several other international students on a tour of the dorms, he learned from the dorm staff that I had checked into the dorms.

Hence, he was at my door with several students and some peer advisors (the new international students' campus familiarization tour) in tow.

When I informed him that not only had I made it to the University, I had already registered for classes and got my student ID and got a job, he was thoroughly flabbergasted.

The only thing he managed to say was, "But we are going to teach you how to do all of this at the new international student orientation tomorrow."

"Then I guess I do not need to attend the orientation," I quipped.

What can I say; I have always been a little bit of a smart ass.

Some of the international students, that were accompanying the Dean as part of the tour, overheard snippets of this conversation and soon several rumors began about the British international student who not only got to the university but also...

As with all rumors, it grew wilder with each go around. When this rumor finally completed the full circle and made its way back to me a few weeks later, it had morphed so far from reality that I had to chuckle. A French student with whom I had developed an acquaintance, came up to me while I was working the access monitor job and said, "Did you hear about the Brit who registered for classes, found a job, slept with someone at the dorms, and found a girlfriend; all in one day."

She continued, "I was just wondering, since you are from the UK, if you know this guy. I would sure like to meet him."

It took all I had not to burst out laughing. I kept a straight face, sighed and said, "No I do not know that person."

I must mention here that I have experienced first-hand how an addiction begins. I have fallen down that spiral. It always starts with one small taste. You just want to see what it feels like. You promise yourself that this is just a one-time thing. You believe in your heart that you are strong and will not get sucked in. However, before you know it you are hooked.

Why did I write the preceding paragraph here? Honestly, I do not know. Remember what I said about a well-structured book or lack thereof. The thought just occurred to me and I could not think of a better placement.

Getting back to college and my education, I have mixed feelings about college life. For the most part, it was pretty mundane and uneventful interspersed with a few flings and trysts. OH! In addition, I must mention the occasional linguistic faux pas that inevitably happens when trying to employ the colloquialisms of the Queen's English in America. One particular example stands out so vividly in my mind that I have to mention it here.

I met this attractive, blonde woman named Wendy. I have a fondness for blue-eyed blonde-haired women. Anyway, we got to talking and I asked her out on a date. She agreed and asked me to pick her up at her dorm room at seven.

In parting, I turned to her and said, "I will come by and knock you up at seven."

I wish you were there to see the color on her face and her expression. I cannot put it into words.

"What," she almost screamed, "What did you just say?"

"I will come by and knock you up at seven." I repeated.

"Just what do you mean by that?" she asked indignantly.

Seeing the expression on her face, I realized that I had unintentionally said something unacceptable and told her what I meant. I was going to come by and knock on her door at seven.

In London, we say, "I'll come by and knock you up at x o'clock…"

Thankfully, she understood that I was not trying to be offensive and explained want "knocking someone up" meant in America. It was my turn to go red in the face. I had several similar incidents with colloquial expressions, but none worth mentioning here.

Four years went by as if in a flash. I guess time passes very quickly when you are having fun and you have very few responsibilities. I fared well at school and graduated with honors. Having completed my bachelor's degree, I decided to pursue my master's degree.

Getting a master's degree was always a lifetime goal. Both my parents have master's degrees. Just two more years of college and then I'll go back home, I told myself. I appeared for my GRE exams and fared well. I decided to stay in Cleveland since I had made several friends by now.

The long summer proved fateful. I had secured admission to the master's degree program. However, I only received a research assistantship. Unlike a full scholarship, a RA-ship pays for your tuition and only your tuition. It does not cover room and board. This meant that I had to find a real job to pay for my room and board and other incidental expenses. This proved to be my downfall.

Most master's degree program classes at Cleveland State University are held in the evening. Therefore, I was free to work during the day. I secured a job as a retail sales associate at an electronics retail chain store. As I mentioned earlier, I did not want to go through the legal rigmarole and ass kissing involved in getting permission to use actual names of organizations where I worked. Therefore, I am using fictitious names. Let us just call this chain "The Audio Chuck."

I began working at the Audio Chuck for minimum wage plus commissions. Again, I promised myself that this was just until I got my master's degree. "Just two years" I said to myself. The way the compensation plan on this job worked was that you were paid minimum wage for your shift and if you sold at an average rate of more than sixty-five dollars per hour for the pay period, you received one percent of your total sales as commission. If you sold at an average rate of more than eighty-five dollars per hour, you made two percent and so on…

Since I did not need a whole lot of money, I promised myself I was going to be content by just doing the minimum. When I got on that sales floor after three days of training, I initially kept my promise to myself. That lasted for two or three weeks. I just hung in there did the bare minimum and minded my own business. No pressure!

Then I noticed that at the end of every month the store manager put up a ranking of the sales persons dollar per hour figures for the month. I had noticed the sheet of paper pinned to the corkboard in the back of the store but had given it very little attention. Now it jumped out at me every time I went to the back of the store. My name was dead last.

That was all it took. My type 'A' personality would not allow me to be the last at anything. Simply put, I went berserk on the sales floor. I sensed the competition.

Something deep within me drove me to prove that I was better than everyone else was.

I have always possessed the ability to be eloquent and charming when I wanted. I worked my natural charm on that sales floor. They used to say back home that I had kissed the Blarney Stone one time too many.

I am certain that all of you have heard about the Blarnery stone. However, just in case, five miles north-west of the small city of Cork is the village of Blarney. Near the village, standing almost ninety feet high is the castle of Blarney. Cormac MacCarthy erected the present castle in 1446. This is the third castle constructed at that site.

Built on a rock, above several caves, the tower originally had three floors. On the top floor, just below the battlements on the parapet, is the world famous Blarney Stone. This stone supposedly gives the gift of eloquence to all who kiss it. I do not know how long this custom has been practiced or how it originated.

Let us get back to the sales floor in the store. I have always possessed the gift of gab. I used this gift to charm everyone who came into that store. Having a foreign accent helped me a lot too. Most women commented that my accent was cute. As a result, I soon had a small following of clients that would come to the store and specifically ask for me.

The store manager was happy with my performance because he made commissions on the overall sales for the entire store.

Suddenly all I could think about was work. I loved going to work every day for the challenge and the competition. I had to see for myself on a daily basis if I could exceed the sixty-five dollars per hour cut-off point and make commission. Little did I know that the drug called Corporate America and the rat race had started gradually ensnaring me? I just had my first taste and I already wanted more.

It is almost like the toad in the hot water experiment. If you throw a toad in hot water, he will instantly jump out. However if you put him in water at room temperature and gradually raise the temperature of the water, he will stay in there until he cooks and dies. I know it sounds cruel. I have not performed this experiment myself. I have read about it in other books and scientific journals.

Anyway, I consistently sold over the sixty-five dollars per hour mark and sometimes even crossed the highest mark of a hundred and twenty-five dollars per hour. For the next four months, I was the number one sales associate in the store. My name was always on the top of the list and I was proud of my achievement. However, achieving is the easy part, it seems. Maintaining the top ranking month after month is quite another ball game. Therefore, I began to work harder and longer just to keep my name at the top.

I had unconsciously begun formulating a work schedule and a lifestyle that would consume me over the next twenty years. I woke up every morning at five am, shaved, showered, made a short work of my ablutions and got two hours of studying done.

I worked from eight am to four thirty pm. I attended classes from five pm to nine pm. I would then go back to my dorm room and study for another hour or two. I tried to go to bed at a decent time so that I could wake up and repeat my routine all over again.

My sales successes came to the attention of the district manager. He initially noticed a jump in average sales per hour number at the store where I worked. When he looked at the store's detailed reports, he noticed that I was consistently outselling the other sales associates at that store.

He casually dropped in to have a chat with me. I learned later that he wanted to interview me and size me up without making it a formal meeting.

I must have said all the right things or at least the things he wanted to hear. After a short conversation, he offered me a chance to join the management trainee program. I was a little reluctant at first until he mentioned that this was a salaried position and I would automatically receive a minimum of one percent commission on all my sales regardless of the dollars per hour threshold. Of course, the higher dollar per hour thresholds still paid a higher commission. I accepted.

From that day forward, I had to attend management trainee classes for four hours every Saturday at the district office. This was in addition to the hours I worked at the store, and the classes I attended at the University.

The district always had six management trainees in the program at any given time ready to step up and take over should any store manager quit or be terminated. They also maintained a monthly ranking list for the management trainees.

Typically, when a store needed a new manager, the management trainee that was consistently at the top of the list for the preceding six months received the promotion. He or she had to fill the store manager slot that had become available. It only took me two months to get my name at the top of that list and I made sure that it stayed at the top. I consistently outpaced every other management trainee in the district.

A few months later, a store became available in the district. I learned later that the store manager was asked to resign because the store was showing declining sales for several months in a row. I was offered the opportunity to run this store as the store manager. I gladly accepted the position and the raise that it entailed.

As a part of the management trainee program, I learned many interesting things about, retail store management, Audio Chuck's management style, etc. In my mind, the most important thing I learned was that in addition to salary and commission on store sales, store managers received additional compensation for maintaining certain levels of profitability.

Most store managers worked the best hours and gave the worst hours to the sales people. I was so determined to be the best that I ran the store with one less sales associate than was allocated in the store budget. I worked all the worst hours and covered what would have been the missing sales associate's shifts.

I was very successful that first year. I personally sold over two hundred thousand dollars of pieces and parts in one calendar year at the Audio Chuck. Only twenty other individuals managed to achieve this feat nationwide. As a reward for our performance, each of us received a certificate and a spun English pewter tankard with our respective names and the words "Two Hundred Thousand Club" engraved. I still have my tankard. It now serves as a mute reminder of my foolishness.

It goes without saying, that as a result of spending all my time at the store, I did not fare too well in my master's degree program. The straight A's of years yonder were gone. They were replaced by several B's and even the occasional C.

After I graduated, I continued to work at the Audio Chuck for another year. I had become known in my district as the 'turnaround kid' and the district manager's favorite hit man. Every time there was a store that showed declining profits, I was sent there to replace the manager. Lo and behold in a few months, the store would be profitable again.

Here is how I did it. I usually identified the sales associate that was performing at the lowest dollar per hour ratio based on the previous six-month average and terminated him or her immediately. I did not hire a sales associate to fill in that floater position. Instead, I scheduled myself to work those hours. I gladly worked long hours, short staffed just because I felt that I had something to prove. After all, I was the 'turnaround kid.' I could not afford to fail as I had a rep to protect.

While I was still at Cleveland State University, in my master's program, I got married. I will tell you the details of my marriage later in this book. I also put a down payment on a small house one block away from Lake Erie. It was a quaint little two-bedroom one and half bathroom brick bungalow.

I was a store manager. I had a house. I was proud of my accomplishments. However, I wanted just that little bit more. The American dream was almost within my grasp. So I naively thought.

The thoughts of going back home to Romford were

banished from my mind forever. I was here to stay. Here, I had become a 'somebody'. I was the 'turn-around kid'. They could not do without me and I could not do without them. I had to be there every day to stay ahead and prove that I still had what it takes. I lived to bask in the glory of knowing that I was wanted and needed. It was a kind of adrenaline rush that I cannot accurately describe in words. You have to feel it to know it.

I was thoroughly and completely hooked. I had become a full-fledged addict without realizing it. I had become a corporate rat race junkie.

Addiction to Corporate America

I continued working at Audio Chuck chasing my American dream that always seemed just beyond my grasp. When I got the house, I wanted a new car. When I got the car, I wanted a better car. Then I wanted a larger house and the big screen TV.

The list kept growing and I kept working harder to keep up with the financial pressures that I put on myself. All the while, I kept promising myself that this one last thing would be enough. I believed that after I achieved whatever this latest need was, I would be content.

Let me tell you folks, once you are hooked, it is extremely difficult if not impossible to stop and let go without some external force acting as a catalyst. It is just as Sir Isaac Newton said, "a body will remain in its state of rest or inertia until displaced by an external force." I know he said that about the principles of physics. However, I believe that it also applies in this context.

What I am trying to say is that once you are hooked on the corporate rate race, everything else in the world seems surreal to you. It typically takes some drastic event, or in some cases more than one drastic event, in your life to shake you from that state and bring you back to reality.

I was far from being disturbed from my state of inertia. I was still climbing the corporate ladder and enjoying it very much. I caught my big break in Corporate America when a man came into my Audio Chuck store looking for some batteries. I struck up a conversation with him and learned that he was on travel. I also learned that he was a vice president for a very large, well-known corporation.

Let us refer to this company as 'LDD' for the purposes of this book. We started chatting and when he learned of my engineering education, he seemed perplexed at what I was doing at a retail store.

He suggested that I interview at LDD. He felt confident that I would do well at the interviews and get hired as a project manager. He actually knew of some government contracts the company had ongoing at Wright Patterson Air Force Base in Dayton, Ohio. He was certain that these programs desperately needed good project managers with strong people skills.

I was skeptical about making this change until he mentioned the base salary for project managers at LDD. It did not take long for me to make up my mind to interview at LDD. I had found out that the base salary paid to project managers at LDD was twice my base salary at Audio Chuck. Furthermore, LDD offered performance based bonuses that were paid on a quarterly basis.

I was sure that once I had this job, with the extra money I made at LDD, I would have everything I ever wanted. I put on my best game face and went to a series of interviews with LDD. Whatever I said at these interviews must have impressed them. Either that or they were a lot more desperate than the vice president described to me.

I was hired at a base salary that was two thousand dollars more than what the VP had mentioned. I began working for LDD. Shortly thereafter, I got an email from the human resources department asking me if I had any objections to filling out an SF-86 form in order to apply for a security clearance.

I had no knowledge of anything related to a security clearance. I did not even know what a security clearance was. I did not know how and where to begin. Therefore, I started asking questions. I learned that the US Department of Defense issued clearances to people after performing a background investigation. Receiving these clearances authorized people to work on classified projects and systems and further granted these individuals access to classified information.

I had, since my marriage, given up my British citizenship and received my American citizenship. I had sworn allegiance to the flag of the United States of America and I was determined to achieve the American dream. The clearance could only enhance my ability to achieve my American dream and getting a clearance seemed like the "in-thing" at LDD, at that time.

My entire life history was reasonably straightforward, uncomplicated and clean with the exception of a few fistfights as a kid in high school. Where I grew up, if a boy did not get into the occasional fistfight in high school, his peers looked down upon him.

I received the security clearance and began working with military clients at Wright Patterson Air Force base. I worked on several exciting programs that I cannot discuss in any detail. It was truly a great ego boost. I was working on classified programs. Not only was I chasing my American dream with vigor. I was also simultaneously serving my adopted country.

This made me feel even more important and was a much bigger rush that just working for Corporate America. When people asked me what I did for a living, I was proudly able to say that it was military stuff and that it was classified.

When I joined LDD, they had mentioned that a typical workweek was forty-five hours. They also mentioned that most project managers worked more than that. I smirked at the hours. After all, I was covering all kinds of hours at the Audio Chuck. A forty-five to fifty hour week would be a vacation. I was not afraid of the long hours.

I do not remember working a single forty-five hour week for my entire tenure at LDD. It was usually fifty-five to sixty hours and sometimes more. In addition, I was salaried so I did not get monetary compensation for the extra hours that I worked. I convinced myself that I was just proving my worth, paying my dues at the new company, in a manner of speaking.

My willingness to slave for LDD with no regard to my family life or any work life balance resulted in my being promoted faster than my peers were. I also made the quarterly performance based bonuses that they had discussed with me when I interviewed. I progressed from project manager to senior project manager to program manager. The raises and bonuses kept rolling in and my needs grew with each raise. That elusive American dream was always there in front of me, always just out of reach.

I was unknowingly paying a high price for all this in terms of my physical health and emotional wellbeing. With each raise and each new position came added responsibility and additional work hours. However, I ate it all up and I wanted more.

The highlight of this phase of my life was getting to know and work with many wonderful military personnel and I made several very good friends. These folks are truly a rare breed. Over the years, I have developed tremendous respect for what they do and the personal sacrifices they make.

Military personnel's salaries are lower when compared to private sector employees. Nevertheless, because of their tremendous love and intense dedication to our country, these man and women are willing to go wherever they are deployed. These brave men and women are willing to fight and die just so that people like you and I can sleep soundly at night knowing that we are safe.

I also greatly admire the dedication of the military spouses. I do not know if I would personally ever be able cope with having a spouse that could be sent off to fight a war at any given instant, sometimes with very little notice.

I have stayed in touch with almost all the military personnel that I met over the years. Some of them have even become life-long friends and confidants.

Let us shift our focus back to my work. My work hours had grown into something horrendous. I was living to work. At the time however, I had no regrets. All this seemed like a logical extension of my natural abilities. I thought and believed that I was utilizing the skills and gifts that God has blessed me with to their fullest extent.

I just wanted to work and achieve. When I achieved what I had set out to achieve, I wanted more. I had become a very shallow and materialistic person. There was always that one last thing I needed, so I worked harder to achieve what I had convinced myself I so desperately needed. It was a vicious downward spiral and I was spiraling out of control.

My work had consumed my life and become my obsession. I kept going on and on until it consumed me completely. Work was all I could think about all the time. I wanted to work more so that I could make that next level, get that next raise, and get that next promotion, make more money so that I could buy that next new thing that had caught my fancy.

When I was a program manager, I wanted the title of director. When I was director, I wanted to be vice president. I enjoyed the power that work gave me. I started going in to work on the weekends.

My work hours had become obscene to say the least. I usually got up at five am. Then, after a quick shower and shave, I left for work. I got to work no later than six am. I worked until six pm at least, sometimes longer and I came home exhausted. Sixty and seventy hour workweeks had become the norm. Eighty plus hour workweeks were not uncommon either, if you counted the hours I put in over the weekend.

When I got home, I was usually famished because I

more often than not did not take a break for lunch. Not enough time you see! So when I got home, I typically took another shower, ate food, watched may be about a half hour of TV and went to bed (passed out from exhaustion would be a more appropriate term).

I did all this just to wake up when the alarm sounded, so that I could repeat it all over again. I wonder why people call it the rat race. I think the hamster race would have been a more appropriate term for what I was doing to myself.

I was like the hamster that keeps running in place on the wheel and makes absolutely no forward progress. Moreover, the faster I ran, the faster the wheel turned. Consequently, I had to run even faster to keep from falling off. Since, that was the only life I knew and I was afraid of falling off, I ran faster. It was a seemingly never-ending cycle.

On the weekends, I usually went in to work for at least four to six hours. Moreover, when I was not at work, I was plugging away at my laptop. This just describes my regular days when I was working in town.

It was a completely different ball game when I traveled. I worked on the airplane, I worked in the airport, and I worked in my hotel room barely stopping to swallow down some room service from time to time. I had become one of those people you often see at airports sitting in some corner with a cell phone to their ear, a laptop computer on their lap and an open brief-case with papers spilling out, oblivious to the world.

On the plane, I was usually curt and sometimes down-right rude to my fellow passengers. I rarely introduced myself to the person next to me. I always got the aisle seat thanks to airline frequent flyer status. I used to sigh, huff and mutter under my breath when the person sitting in either the middle or window seat wanted me to move so that they could use the restroom.

I acted as if I owned the plane and like my co-passengers normal bodily functions were a major inconvenience to me. I guess at that time, I blinded myself to the fact that they had paid for a ticket just like me. I sometimes think of the number of people I offended and was rude to on plane rides and it makes me sad.

I remember this one incident on a flight from Phoenix Sky Harbor International Airport to Washington Dulles. As soon as the person next to me took their seat, I turned to them and said, "I hope you are not one of those people who likes to talk on planes, I have tons of work to accomplish." Yes, I know, I was incredibly rude.

I now think of the countless opportunities I missed to interact with other human beings and regret my actions. I could have shared a light conversation or a small laugh with thousands of other human beings. However, I lost that opportunity.

I believed at the time that I was above other travelers. I was after all one of those elite people who carry the gold or platinum status card on airlines and hotels. I envied the people that had a higher frequent flyer or hotel rewards status. I always wanted to achieve that next higher status.

The airlines and hotels also seem to do all they can to promote this divide. There is a separate line for people who have elite status. The airlines and hotels give their frequent guests preferential treatment and make them feel extra special.

Such was my naïveté at the time that I thought they did all this because I was special. I was special to the hotels and airlines all right, just as long as I continued to spend money on airline tickets and hotel stays. When I stopped traveling, in the eyes of the hotels and airlines, I became just like the countless other people that I thought were beneath me.

The price that I paid to get and keep these elite statuses was very high. I was away from home. I did not have time to spend with the people that should have meant the most to me. Nowadays when I see any of these elite travelers, I cannot help but feel a small hint of sadness for them and the price that they may have paid in their personal lives to achieve that status.

The glamour of the consulting lifestyle had me completely brainwashed. I had once heard a story of a consultant who worked for one of the big six consulting firms. Apparently, this young woman received a call from a client at one am on her cell phone. It startled her and being in an unfamiliar hotel room, she tripped as she got out of bed to answer her phone. It is said that she fractured her left arm as a result of the fall.

The story goes. She answered the phone call, booted up her computer and took care of the client's issue typing with her right hand before calling for help to get to a hospital for her fractured arm.

At the time while I was still high on consulting, I thought what she did was amazing. She was the ideal consultant. For a while after that, this consultant, a person who I had never met was my idol.

I guess when a person is so fully addicted to something, (in this case Corporate America); they never see the down side. I believed it was all peaches and cream. All the while, I was paying a high personal price by compromising my health and happiness.

However, the persons that paid the highest price are my friends and loved ones. In order to support my addiction and experience that one more thrill or achieve that one more goal, I neglected and ignored the ones that should have meant the most to me. I neglected the people that loved me and stood by my side…

I married my first wife Bridgit, when we both were very young. She was of Irish and Sicilian decent. She was three-quarters Irish and one-quarter Sicilian, to be precise. Describing her as a fiery combination would be a gross understatement.

I met her in college. I was just completing my master's and she was completing her bachelor's. I liked her fire, passion and unpredictability. She liked my resolve, drive and steadfastness. We were true opposites in every sense of the word.

It started out as a simple platonic friendship but as our conversations grew deeper, so did our fondness for each other. Liking grew to longing and longing to loving. Soon we were spending every spare waking moment with each other. We were still in our early twenties when we got married.

I was enamored by her and by the thought of being married. The first few months of our marriage were blissful. Money was always short. However, we had some good times together. We enjoyed the simple pleasures like going to the pond and feeding breadcrumbs to the ducks, cooking on the grill in the middle of a snowstorm and other crazy things.

However, this bliss was short-lived. Over the next few years, we grew further and further apart. I got sucked into the rat race and my work life became more important than my personal life. I would rather be at work than spend quality time at home with Bridgit.

I wanted to stay in hotels and fly on airlines so that I could achieve the elite statuses. I yearned to say that I am a hundred thousand mile flyer or a platinum hotel guest. All the wrong things were more important to me than the woman I had promised to love honor and cherish.

I craved the corporate attention and recognition. I lived for the scraps of praise and recognition that Corporate America threw my way. I liked the fact that I could go to work and when I came home, all I needed to say was that it was classified. It was a feeling of power, an ultimate high. I was wedded more to my work that to my wife.

I found out the hard way that marriages do not flourish or last because one person is on a power trip. Maintaining any relationship is very hard daily work. Marriage requires both persons to contribute their fair share. My mother often told me her opinions about marriage while I was growing up.

"It takes two hands to clap," she would say.

She was trying to impress upon my young mind, the importance of both persons in a relationship participating equally. I had heard my mom's words, but did not follow her advice.

I would be gone traveling for weeks on end, come back home to drop off my bags and then head out to the office. I realize now that I neglected to put in even a small fraction of the time and effort that I gladly gave to my work in my marriage. Sure, I did all the right things materialistically. I brought home the flowers, the jewelry, the expensive cars, the expensive bottles of perfume and so on.

However, I did not give Bridgit the most important things in a marriage. I had not given her the warmth, the compassion, the love and the sense of belonging that makes a relationship work. How could I? I belonged to Corporate America mind, body and soul.

It was just a matter of time before it happened. I came home from one of my many business trips and got the shock of my life. Bridgit informed me that she was seeing someone else. I was furious. I wanted to tear the world apart, I wanted revenge, I wanted…

I did not do any of those things. Instead, I contacted a lawyer almost immediately and filed for a divorce. She did not contest. She signed the papers, packed her bags and left. I learned later that she relocated to Dallas, Texas, where she still resides. She has rebuilt her life and found someone else. Above all, she is happy.

Nevertheless, what do you think I did while this was happening?

If you said work, you guessed right. I worked. Since there was no longer a reason for me to go home at all, I was free to spend every waking moment at my work. I reasoned that work was my solace. Moreover, it kept me from brooding over my home life that was in ruins.

I was certain that hard work would help me make it through this bad period in my life. How could she do this to me? What if I did not have my work to fall back on? Where would I be now? I grew more thankful that I had my work to keep me occupied. I did not realize at the time that my work was the cause of my problems at home and not my savior.

I have heard that addicts always go back to the source of their addiction for relief and that this helps them to forget the worries of the world. I did exactly that, I went back and immersed myself in my work. I worked and worked and then I worked some more. At work, I was a 'somebody.' The price I had paid in my home life only served to enhance my value at work.

Let me tell you something folks, Corporate America loves a slave. That is exactly what I had become. My addiction to the rat race had made me a slave to my work. I worked without care for my health or myself.

Corporate America rewarded me for my lack of a personal life. I received many promotions as a result. First, I became director, then senior director and finally vice president. Bigger titles came with their own baggage in the form of added responsibility and more work.

Sure, I had a few casual flings here and there but nothing remotely long term or serious. I did not have the time to be tied down. I would proudly mention my titles and the hours I worked, to everyone I met, as if it were a badge of honor or something similar.

I must mention here that even though it took a few years following our divorce, I eventually realized that Bridgit was only human and she did what she did out of loneliness and because I was completely ignoring her. She needed human contact, warmth and compassion.

Bridgit in turn also realized how much she had hurt me. Subsequently, Bridgit and I reached a stage of mutual understanding, forgave each other and moved on. We trade emails occasionally and keep each other abreast of our separate lives. That is pretty much the story of my first marriage.

Let me tell you about my second marriage.

I was so completely enamored with my corporate identity and so full of myself that I almost blew my only chance to be with the love of my life and my soul mate Patricia.

Here is how this episode in my life unfolded.

A good friend called me on my cell phone and told me that she wanted to introduce me to someone that very evening. It was a Friday morning and I happened to be at San Francisco International airport waiting for my flight back to Washington Dulles International Airport when I got that phone call.

I will tell you about my relocation from Cleveland, Ohio to Washington, DC in a later chapter.

When I got this phone call from my friend, my first reaction was to decline. However, she insisted, harangued, cajoled and nagged me into agreeing. Yes she did all of those things. I am not exaggerating. I often think back to that conversation and silently thank my friend for all that arm-twisting.

Over the years, Patricia turned out to be my pillar of strength. She is the rock that has stood by my side through hell and high water. She is the rock that has been the source of my strength through many challenging times. I know that she will be by my side no matter what my circumstances.

Let us get back to the phone call that I received while at San Francisco airport. After a five-hour flight, I reluctantly stopped by my friend's office on my way home from Washington Dulles airport. I did it because I had promised my friend that I would. However, when I entered her office, my eyes were treated to a feast.

Sitting in a chair was one of the most gorgeous women that I had ever laid eyes on. She was a petite woman with beautiful blue eyes, long blonde hair and an angelic face. She stood just over five feet tall. I guessed she must have weighed all of a hundred pounds, if that.

Nevertheless, she had an aura about her that made her seem almost ethereal. Her voice was melodious and soothing. She had about her a kind of energy that was all at once intriguing, entrancing and sensual.

Any man would be lucky to have her. I am certain that most men would have gladly given their right arm to be with her. I have already mentioned my fondness for blue-eyed blonde-haired women in previous chapters of this book.

By all counts, I should have fallen head over heels at the very sight of her. However, I did nothing of the sort. I did quite the opposite. I was so caught up in the corporate world and my own egocentric fantasies that I was actually cold and rude to her.

My friend introduced Patricia as a very gifted artist and muralist. In my mind, I thought that a bachelor's degree in studio arts was only good for flipping burgers.

I was certain that Patricia barely made ends meet with her art no matter how talented. Surely, she was beneath me I reasoned. After all, I was the corporate consulting powerhouse, the golden boy. I know, I know, I full of myself in those days!

I coldly shook hands, informed Patricia, and my mutual friend (who has asked to remain anonymous – no fictitious name for her either) who introduced us that I had important classified work that needed my attention. I then left my friend's office in a hurry almost as if the very sight of Patricia repulsed me.

I am sure that I left two very bewildered women back in that office. Both of them probably questioned my sanity or my vision or both.

Later that night after working many more hours, I returned home to my empty Condo. I began reminiscing on my day and started having second thoughts about my actions that day. A small voice inside me said, "what if she was the one?"

I mulled over this for a little while and could not seem to get her blue eyes, blonde hair and beautiful face from my mind. It was as if she had cast a spell on me in that brief meeting. "Too late," I thought to myself and sighed; "but at least I have my work to keep me busy."

In the meantime, unbeknownst to me, Patricia had formed the accurate impression that I was an arrogant snob and did not want to have anything to do with me. However, she later admitted that she had also found something about me to be very intriguing also.

Then thankfully, fate took a hand...

I mentioned my move from Cleveland, Ohio to Washington, DC earlier. This is how it happened. LDD Corporation was involved in a hostile takeover. Our management did not want it to happen. We fought valiantly for almost six months against it. However, in the end, we lost the war.

The Monday after the takeover, I went into work expecting business as usual with some minor changes that would not affect me. I found out soon that I was very naive and dead wrong. I completely unprepared for what I encountered. As I walked up to the office building, there was a line of employees at the front door.

Two persons I had never seen prior to that day blocked the doors. They asked individuals to identify themselves before entering the building. They were checking names against two clipboards that they held in their hands.

It did not take me long to noticed a pattern. Non-management personnel were allowed to enter the building and proceed to their regular office workspace. However, everyone with a title of senior director and above was directed to the main conference room.

Since I held the title of vice president, I was one of the people who had to go to the main conference room.

A couple of legal types met us in the conference room and they offered each of us a six-month severance package if we voluntarily resigned. Alternatively, we could opt to stay on with the new management and take our chances.

I was lost and unsure of what to do. My boss the senior divisional vice president must have noticed the confusion written all over my face.

He walked up to me and whispered in my ear; "take the package," and so I did.

I walked out of that room in a daze. Corporate America and the company to whom I had so lovingly given my blood, sweat and tears had just cast me out. I was uncertain of my next steps and for the first time since I began this journey, I was afraid and confused.

However, the same wind that slams one door shut almost always blows another door open. Some venture capitalist types (VCs hereafter) had heard about what I had accomplished with LDD. They approached me within days of my being laid off from LDD with an interesting offer.

They had just invested heavily in a company in Cleveland, Ohio and acquired controlling interest. This company needed a strong operations person to run the professional services division. Let us call this company P & Q Systems (P & Q hereafter).

If I had any sense, I would have taken some time off since I had six months of severance. I could have visited my parents in London. I could have travelled. I could have done many things. However, I had already been out of work for a week and desperately needed my corporate fix. Therefore, I jumped at the opportunity and joined P & Q as the vice president of professional services.

I immediately set about doing what I did best. I began making all the changes that I felt necessary to drive up profitability. As usual, I stuck to my tried and true modus operandi. I fired several individuals because I felt they did not perform to the high standards that I expected in my staff. I hired on people that were willing to devote their every waking minute to the corporation.

I was directly propagating the mentality of Corporate America that had enslaved me by hiring people just like me who wanted to be slaves to Corporate America. While at the same time, I was firing people that wanted to maintain a reasonable work-life balance. The result was exactly as expected. I drove the profitability up and the costs down. The VCs were extremely happy with my performance.

To this day, I remember the drama that happened while firing this one person, Irene. When I told her that I no longer needed her services and I was terminating her, she started bawling. She told me about how she was

---

a single mother raising three kids and how much she needed the job. She sobbed about how she was willing to do what it takes, work harder, and so on. Little did I care?

All I cared about was the bottom line, the P&L and making the VCs happy. I was the 'Golden Boy'; I had to make a profit. I did not care how. I was completely oblivious to the human factor in the equation at that time and for several more years to come. Even when, on her way out, Irene called me a heartless bastard, it did not register. I had convinced myself that I was doing the right thing for the bottom line.

I realize now how far I had fallen without knowing or caring at the time. Gone was the Atul who had kissed the Blarney Stone. Corporate America had slowly suffocated the sweet eloquent, affable person, who once was well-liked by everyone he met. That person had died a slow but sure death.

A cold corporate killer that found the P&L and bottom line to be more important than human emotions had taken up residence in the body of the cheerful bubbly boy from Romford. I had reached the ultimate low point in my life. At the time, I was completely oblivious this fact also.

True to my addiction, I worked hard ignoring all else until the company made it to the point where the VCs wanted to sell it. Being the good corporate soldier, I complied. I actually helped broker a deal, under the terms of which our primary competitor brought all the assets of P & Q Systems.

When I mention the word 'assets,' I am referring to the software, the intellectual property and rights to the products, not the people. A few software architects and engineers that helped conceptualize the product line stayed on. However, the rank and file of the personnel were let go. Yes, I was once again responsible for getting over fifty people laid off. However, I was true to my word in one sense. The VCs made a lot of money. I got a small share of it too.

For the second time in as many years, I was again without a company. This time I did not worry because I knew that the VCs had a plan for me. They asked me if I had any objections moving to Washington, DC. I was told that my clearance, experience and knowledge of the DoD made me an ideal candidate for a position in Washington, DC.

In addition, they had in mind just the right company for me. Funny coincidence, would you not say! Let us call this company 'Serviciality' – fictitious name naturally.

I had traveled to DC several times for business over the past decade and had made some friends there. In the meantime, I had grown distant from my friends in Cleveland during the divorce from Bridgit. I had no real ties to Cleveland anymore. I was freshly divorced, so what did I have to lose?

I put my house on the market, packed my stuff and moved to Washington, DC. Actually to Fairfax in northern Virginia, about twenty-two miles outside DC. I was still very stuck up. I craved the next biggest thing in my American dream. Living in Fairfax County, one of the five highest per capita income counties in the US suited me just fine.

The glamour and power of Northern Virginia and Washington, DC took me by storm and sucked me in further. Here was the seat of world power. Washington, DC was not just the political capital of the USA; it was the political capital of the free world. Moreover, I was walking the corridors of power, rubbing elbows with the DC elite. Generals, Colonels, SES personnel, CIOs of various government agencies, etc. What a power trip! I had reached a new high. However, like a true addiction, it was never enough. I wanted even more.

Working at Serviciality was interesting and fun at first. It was very different from being in Cleveland. I still had a lot to learn about Washington, DC and about the political intricacies and power plays of government contracting. I flourished under the challenge.

I absorbed knowledge from every source that I could find. I read the FAR (Federal Acquisitions Regulations). I scoured the internet and learned all about the SBA programs, the various procurement channels, the GSA (General Services Administration), set-aside contracts, 8A programs and much more. In a short few months, I had assimilated enough knowledge and information that I could pass myself off as an expert once again.

Serviciality was no longer a challenge. It was just like the hundreds of other professional services companies around the Washington DC beltway. These companies, often collectively referred to as the 'Beltway Bandits' scratch out a living by fighting and competing for the myriad of small to medium sized contracts that were procured by various federal government agencies each year.

I decided that being the vice president at a medium sized 'Beltway Bandit' company no longer fulfilled my cravings. As usual, I wanted more. I wanted to play with the big boys and the multi-billion dollar contracts. I cautiously began shopping my resume around the big name companies in government consulting. It took a little time, but eventually, the opportunity I was looking for came to me.

One of the big six management-consulting firms was looking for a consulting executive with the right mix of educational background, experience, and appropriate security clearances to run a multi-year, multi-million dollars per year Federal contract that they had just won. I interviewed, was hired and I jumped ship.

I bid adieu to my VC friends explaining the circumstances and the challenges I needed. They seemed understanding and assured me that should I change my mind I could always come knocking. I remember their parting words. "There is always room for a talented executive like you in our organization."

Let us call the company I joined 'Slavesture Consulting' (Slavesture, hereafter).

It was while I was still working for Slavesture that I met Patricia through our mutual friend.

As I mentioned in an earlier chapter, I was so full of myself and was so high on my corporate identity that I treated her with cold contempt when we were initially introduced to each other. Later that evening when I returned to my empty Condo, I started having second thoughts about my actions. I was certain that I had lost my opportunity to get to know her. I realized that because of my arrogance, I would probably never see her or hear from her again. Then fate took a hand…

A short while after that incident in my anonymous friend's office, I received another phone call. It was from the same friend that had introduced Patricia to me. She informed me that Patricia had managed to fracture her right foot in multiple places as a result of a nasty fall she suffered. Thus, she was unable to drive anywhere.

My friend suggested that I check up on Patricia and see if she needed any help. My friend also informed me that Patricia lived only a mile or so from my Condo. Another small piece of pertinent information that I had failed to elicit when I was first introduced to Patricia.

As luck would have it, I happened to be driving in the direction of Patricia's house. Surely, this was fate, I thought. As soon as my friend told me the name of her street, I turned my vehicle into that neighborhood.

I was full of myself. I was a full-fledged rat race junkie. However, I was certainly not stupid. Opportunity had knocked a second time. Here it was, by virtue of some miracle, the opportunity that I thought I had lost forever. I jumped at this second chance and drove up to the townhouse where Patricia lived. I went up to her door and rang the doorbell.

Patricia seemed more than a little surprised to see me show up at her doorstep unannounced. However, she invited me in. My entrance was punctuated a few seconds later by a frantic phone call from our mutual friend announcing to Patricia that I was on my way over.

Apparently, I was not the only one that liked what I saw at that initial meeting. Patricia later informed me, that she had told our mutual friend that I intrigued her. However, she had concluded that I was an egocentric jerk, because of my behavior at that initial introductory meeting. Consequently, she did not pursue me further.

Her leg was in a cast and would be for another six weeks. I actually took vacation for the first time in decades and set about the task of helping Patricia in her time of need. However, I did have a secondary agenda. I wanted to get to know her better. Seeing her again made me realize how much she had captivated me in the first place.

Over the next several weeks, I spent every waking moment with Patricia. I tended to her every need. I shopped for her groceries. I brought her takeout food. I drove her to the doctor for checkups. I cooked for her. I was very attentive. She however proved to be an enigma that I was not quite prepared to handle at the time.

She told me that she liked wine so I bought her a bottle of Chateau Lafite Rothschild1981. She commented on its smoothness and richness but did not make a big deal. How it could not be a big deal made no sense to me. After all, I had paid several hundred dollars for that one bottle of wine. I assumed that she did not know much about wines.

Therefore, I proceeded to download the wine classifications along with the history of first growths and printed the document. I assumed wrong. When I showed the document to her, she seemed very knowledgeable on the subject of wines and yet unimpressed by the cost of the wine.

I made many similar extravagant gestures with expensive jewelry, gourmet food and expensive perfume. However, none of them had the desired effect on her. In the past women had OO'd and AAH'd over similar gifts and acted as if I had given them the Hope Diamond.

I was dumbfounded at Patricia's responses to my gifts. I realized that I needed help. I asked a longtime friend, Bill Ashton for advice. He suggested flowers.

"What kind of flowers?" I asked.

"I know the florist and I can easily get a big bouquet of rare flowers put together at short notice." I continued.

"Why don't you try plain old roses?" Bill said.

"Just plain old roses, Bill you do not understand she has treated all the expensive gifts as if they were nothing." I said.

"She will probably dump those roses in the trash."

Bill was insistent that I give her plain old roses. Having tried everything that I knew worked in the past, and not having any better ideas myself, I followed Bill's suggestion. I went to my florist and got one dozen plain white long-stem roses.

I was tempted to get three or four dozen, but I fought back the impulse. When I went by that evening with pizza and wine for dinner, I gave the roses to her. Much to my surprise and delight, she was ecstatic. She fawned over those roses as if they were made of gold.

Patricia lit up as if I had suddenly undergone a transformation in her eyes. Like the frog that had suddenly turned into a prince. All this was still a little beyond my comprehension. I went along with the flow. We sat down for dinner (pizza and wine) and for the first time, it seemed like we really talked.

This time, our conversation was not just about the weather and her broken foot. We conversed and connected at a much deeper level. Before we realized it, it was almost dawn. We had talked through the night. It was almost as if a curtain had lifted, a wall had crumbled and she had suddenly seen into my heart. From that moment forward, Patricia took a deep personal interest in me.

She asked me about my collection of art. Apparently, our mutual friend had told Patricia that I had a collection of artworks and some rare books about art. I had collected these over the years. Over those very years, the Atul that reveled in art for its beauty and intrigue began looking at objects of art as status symbols. To me art had become something that I used to brag about and to impress friends and acquaintances. When it came to art, I had become the ultimate cliché.

My addiction to work had suppressed my ability to enjoy art for its own sake. I remember the early days in Europe when I would proudly talk about a Rodin sculpture and its history as if I had carved it myself. However, over the past several years, I presented my collection of art to my friends and acquaintances in the following manner. "Here's a replica of Rodin's Sculpture 'The Kiss' in marble. It cost me eighteen thousand dollars, but it was worth it."

I distinctly remember one night when Patricia continued to dumbfound me with questions like:

- How often do you read the books that you have?
- How often do you touch your art?
- Do you really enjoy what you do?

The more she dug into me, the more I began not to like the person I had become. Had she asked these same questions of the Atul from Romford, I would have had very different answers to all these questions. Once again, we continued our conversation into the wee hours of the morning and then I left. I was sure that we had a very strong connection. However, I was still unsure about what Patricia really thought of me.

Over the next few weeks, our conversations got deeper and we began to understand each other truly. Patricia, as it turned out, is an exceptionally gifted artist. Her paintings and murals are amazingly true to life. When

I first saw some samples of her work, they astounded me and quite literally took my breath away. I was more determined than ever to win her over. However, she always seemed to hover on that boundary-line somewhere between interested and distant.

Finally, I could not take it anymore. I asked her if she did not like me. Her answer stunned me. I was not prepared for it. She said that she actually liked me very much and thought about us all the time. However, she wanted someone who would share her life with her and she did not think I was that person.

"What do you mean I am not that person?" I asked indignantly.

"Have I not taken vacation and been here by your side day after day helping you in your time of need?" I said.

"Sure you have." She replied, "But what happens when you go back to work?"

Those words struck home. She was more correct than even she knew. I was already beginning to miss the corporate world, the feeling of power, the excitement of the rat race. I knew that needed a work-fix and I needed one fast.

At the same time, I was not prepared to lose her and I began to formulate a plan. After a lot of pondering, I came up with a compromise. I told her what she wanted to hear. I told Patricia that I would resign from

Slavesture, since that job that kept me on the road. I also agreed to find another job at a local company so that I would have more time to spend with her.

I promised her this, and she said she believed me. However, I knew deep down that no matter where I went, no matter what company I worked for, I was still not ready to shake of my addiction to the Corporate Rat Race.

I went back to the VCs and told them that I had enough of the Big Six consulting lifestyle and was back at their doorstep to see if they needed my skills. I was ready to take on the next challenge that they could offer. Since I had always made them money in the past, they obliged and seemed to have just the right opportunity for me as usual. Let us call this one "Hyperposes."

Soon thereafter, I joined Hyperposes as a vice president. A short while after that, I asked Patricia to marry me. I wish I could say that my proposal was fancy and romantic. However, that would be a lie. However, I did one thing that delighted Patricia. She had informed me that she liked tanzanite. I had a jeweler create a unique engagement ring with a diamond in the center flanked by heart-shaped tanzanite stones on either side.

When I asked her to marry me, she agreed on one condition. She made me promise that I would spend true quality time with her. She reiterated that that she did not need money or materialistic things to be happy. All she wanted was someone who would share her life with her, be there for her, and make her his number one priority. I promised her that I would. Deep down, I knew fully well that I was making a promise I could not keep.

I had sunk to a completely new low even for me. I had quite literally conned a wonderful person into marrying me...

Our wedding was a quiet affair. Neither of us is very big on pomp and ceremony. We planned a quick trip to Las Vegas. We got married in a simple church ceremony. After the ceremony, we spent four wonderful days together at the Hyatt Regency resort in Henderson, Nevada. This resort is truly like an oasis in the desert.

However, four days flew by as if in the blink of an eye and soon the vacation was over and so was the honeymoon. The other Atul, the cold corporate killer, the corporate rat race junkie reared his ugly head. We both gave up our individual residences and bought a home in Fairfax County, Northern Virginia.

I craved my work fix and that is exactly where I ran back to as soon as we got home. Apparently, it would seem that I had learned nothing from the mistakes of my first marriage. I once again immersed myself in my work. I was back in my element. In a few days, I fell back into my old routine. I began to leave home at five am and worked late almost every day.

I made great strides at Hyperposes. I even won the chairman's award since my division was the most profitable and fastest growing division in the company. As with my past jobs, I did what I did best. I followed my modus operandi to a tee. I cut loose personnel that I thought were the dead weight and replaced them individuals that were willing to work day and night with no concern for their personal life.

The Board of Directors' and VCs were full of praise for my efforts. I was back on my high. I fell back into my old routine very easily. I woke up even earlier. Most days I was up at four thirty am and left the home at five am to beat the DC traffic. I did not come home until after rush hour was over, seven or eight pm at the earliest. In addition, I worked on the weekends.

Through this entire period, I ignored my beautiful bride, Patricia. I had worked very hard to win her affections. However, once I was back in Corporate America, I grew blind to all the qualities that had attracted me to her in the first place.

I forgot to mention earlier. During my tenure at Slavesture, I had enrolled in a doctoral program. This meant that any time that I did not spend working, I spent studying for my PhD. I spent hours on my computer and at the library researching materials for my dissertation.

I had fallen back on my old ways very easily. I brought home expensive gifts, diamond tennis bracelets, jade sculptures, and Italian alabaster artifacts. The list is endless. Once again, I neglected to give Patricia what she needed the most, someone to spend time with her. I gave these expensive gifts to Patricia expecting her to be happy. Instead, with each gift, I could only see a more sadness in Patricia's eyes.

This irritated me and I once even remarked; "No matter what I get you, I can never seem to make you happy."

Her response was; "All I want is for you to spend time with me. I do not need the jewelry or any other gifts."

She suggested that I find another job or start my own business where I worked fewer hours. I pooh-poohed the very idea.

"Where do you think all we have comes from?" I said.

"I work hard so that we can have the big house, the fancy cars, the big screen TV."

Her response was, "Before you came along, I was happy with a small twenty-inch TV."

"How dare she say these things," I thought.

Here I am working hard buying her all these gifts and she does not appreciate me. I left my home in a huff, slammed the door behind me and went right back to my office. I had convinced myself that I was in the right and that she was being unreasonable.

A wise saying goes; "There is none as blind as he who refuses to see." How true.

I was blind to everything else but my addiction to the corporate rat race. I wanted it, I needed it and it had become my identity. At that point, in my life, my work was akin to the very air I breathed. I felt that could live without food, water or love. However, I could not live without the corporate fix.

Matters between Patricia and I took a turn for the worse. If we had any conversation at all, it seemed to end up in an argument. We just could not seem to communicate. At every turn, I thought she was the one in the wrong. I thought that she was being unreasonable.

"True, she was an extremely gifted artist, but art did not pay the bills," I reasoned with myself.

"After all, I made orders-of-magnitude more money than she made."

My addiction had blinded me to the facts. I did not remember then, that before we married, she had told me that all she wanted someone who would share a life with her. She had asked for someone who would make her his number one priority. I did not remember that I had promised her I would be all those things.

To this day, I still cannot fathom how or why Patricia hung in there by my side. Nevertheless, I am very thankful that she did.

These thoughts were furthest from my mind at that time. All I knew was that I was killing myself at work. I convinced myself that I was doing all this for us and Patricia did not see my sacrifice.

My work at Hyperposes was going better than expected. Revenue was up, profitability was even higher and the P&L looked healthy. We had won some large contracts with the Department of Defense. The VCs were certain that Hyperposes would be an attractive M & A (merger and acquisition) target in a few short months. I did my part by trying harder to squeeze every penny of profitability that I could. I worked my managers hard and my employees harder.

The wake-up call came silently, suddenly and inevitably. While at a client site one day, I began to feel discomfort and numbness in my left arm. I thought nothing of it. Muscular spasm I said and continued working. I work out every other day and I am in very good shape for my age. One of my program managers convinced me to leave the client site and home.

"Chief," he said, "you really do not look well. Please go home. I got the client site covered."

I pushed back for a few minutes and then realized that I truly did not feel well.

"Probably just a touch of the flu," I said. However, I took his advice and went home.

When I got home, Patricia got one look at me and drove me straight to the urgent care medical center. The doctor took my blood pressure and refused to let me move until I had taken some medication. He also insisted that I lay down right there on the examining table for half an hour after I had taken the medication.

I heard the doctors discussing with each other. "Did you see the blood pressure on that guy?"

Naturally, I inferred that I was the person they were referring to in that conversation. Apparently, my blood pressure was 196/128 and the doctor was surprised at the fact that I had not suffered a stroke.

To this day, Patricia claims that only the strength of her love and her prayers kept me from having a stroke on that fateful day. What is more intriguing is that I believe her. I truly believe that her prayers and her love for me kept me alive when my blood pressure was so high that my arteries and veins were primed to explode, literally.

However, I was not ready to quit my addiction to Corporate America just yet. The doctor put me on blood pressure medication. I took the medication regularly and I went back to work. I promised Patricia that things were going to change and that I was planning to slow down. Therefore, I took it easy for a week or two. However, that respite was short lived. I soon slipped back into my old work schedule.

Patricia was distraught. She talked to me, reasoned with me, and finally she began to nag me about changing my career. I resisted with all my might. This led to more arguments between us. During the course of one of these arguments, she asked me what would happen if I were to die.

I was so callous that I replied, "If I die, you should have no worries. You will be rich. We have a great life insurance policy on me."

Then Patricia said the words that finally broke through the haze. Somewhere in my clouded, addicted mind, her words registered, albeit for a brief moment. I finally got a fleeting glimpse of what she was trying to get me to understand. The first step in curing any problem is admitting you have a problem.

Almost all at once, great realization filled my very being. I needed to change my life drastically. I realized that I was addicted to my work. I was a slave to Corporate America.

The corporate rat race junkie was ready to try rehab.

I bet you are wondering what Patricia said that awakened me and opened my eyes. I promise, I will tell you.

However, it is now time for our next exercise…

Act

Do you remember the lists? Yes, the same lists that you created when you did the RECOGNIZE exercise.

- One that contains your dream life and per-ceived obstacles.
- The other that contains your skills and capabilities

Please bring them out and place them in front of you. Do you have a pen or pencil handy? Excellent!

Now, let us change the RECGINIZE list slightly. Let us add some text in the middle column. Let us add the words "Here is how I ACT to overcome each obstacle."

Now, start thinking about what actions you need to take in order to overcome each of these obstacles. Let me give you some examples from my personal life.

I had a large mortgage. The action that I took was to sell the large house and move to a smaller house for half the mortgage

I also lived in an area of the country that ranked amongst the top ten in cost of living. The action I took was to relocate to an area which was more moderate in cost of living and yet commutable to where I wanted to work.

These examples mentioned above are specific to my life. Your actions could include relocation, training, changing some habits, accepting a new paradigm, etc.

This exercise is not something you are going to be able to do in five minutes, unless you have already been giving this some serious thought. Once again, I am going to ask you to put down the book and take some time to yourself.

Please bookmark this page.

Spend a few hours thinking about what actions you need to take. Write down everything you can think about on our sheet of paper.

After you are done, your list should look something like this:

My Dream life is _____		
The things I RECOGNIZE that keep me from pursuing my dream life are:	Here is how I ACT to over-come each obstacle:	
- Item 1 - Item 2 - Item 3 - Item 4 - - - -	- Action 1 - Action 2 - Action 3 - Action 4 - - - -	

Now we are going to take this one-step further. We are going to change the sentences in the ACT list by adding a realistic timeline to them and converting them into affirmations. It is very easy to convert something to an affirmation, just start your sentence with, I AM.

I AM doing this to achieve this goal. A note of caution, you should not have the words "I will not" in your list. We do not focus on the negative, not now or ever. How do we accomplish this? Simple!

If you have written down, "I **will not** spend excessively beyond my budget." Convert it to, "I **AM** always living within my budget." OR

If you have written down, "I **will not** procrastinate."

Convert it to, "I **AM** always performing tasks in a time-ly manner"

This was another valuable lesson that my father taught me. He told me it was best to put things in a positive light or perspective. He elaborated by saying that it was the difference between telling someone that 'all their relatives will die before them' versus telling them that 'they would live the longest amongst all their relatives.'

For some reason, the words that my dad told me when I was thirteen or fourteen years old, have stuck with me in my head. Both statements essentially mean the same thing. The former is depressing and negative. However, the latter is uplifting and positive.

Secondly, goals and objectives are not complete until they meet the SMART criteria. I know, you are prob-ably wondering what I mean by SMART?

SMART is an acronym, it stands for Specific, Measurable, Acceptable, Realistic and Time-bound. I am not going to delve deep into goal creation here. If you are interested in finding out more about goals and objectives, I request you to read my book "Goals-Based Strategic Planning."

Let us discuss some examples. I mentioned earlier that I had planned to sell my house and move to a smaller house.

I could say, "It is <pick the next working day/date> and I AM in a smaller house with a smaller mortgage because I sold my large house."

Ask yourself, does this statement meet the SMART criteria?

Yes, it is specific, measurable, and time-bound. It may be acceptable to someone if his or her house is already prepped for sale. However, is it realistic?

Think about it, the typical time line from accepting an offer to closing on a sale for a house is thirty days.

Giving time for prepping, listing, showing, seasonal variances, etc., an appropriate statement might be, "It is <pick a day/date approximately three months from now> and I AM in a smaller house with a smaller mortgage because I sold my large house."

Now let us take this one-step further.

Let us add some text in the right column of the RECOGNIZE-ACT list. Let us add the words "The skills and knowledge that help me with these actions are."

Remember the list of knowledge, skills and capabilities that you RECOGNIZED. Please bring it out and match up the skills you have to actions that they will help support.

My Dream life is _____

The things I RECOGNIZE that keep me from pursuing my dream life are:	Here is how I ACT to overcome each obstacle:	The skills and knowledge that help me with these actions are:
- Item 1	- Action 1	- Skill 1
- Item 2	- Action 2	- Skill 2
- Item 3	- Action 3	- Skill 3
- Item 4	- Action 4	- Skill 4
-	-	-
-	-	-
-	-	-
-	-	-

Please remember that the relationship between actions and skills is a many-to-many non-exclusive relationship. This means that you may have many skills associated with a particular action or you may have many actions associated with a particular skill.

It is also possible that you may have some skills that do not match up to an action or you may have some actions that do not have associated skills. This is also fine.

At the end of this exercise, you should have a concrete list of actions that you need to take in order to actualize your dream life. Now all you have to do is **ACT**.

This does not mean you have to do it all at once. I understand that we cannot leap over mountains in one single leap. However, if you take one-step at a time and keep taking the next step, you will eventually reach the top and be able to cross over to the other side.

Do not focus on the top of the mountain. That may seem faraway or at times unattainable. ACT, instead, on achieving the next step and just the next step. Once you take that step, ACT on the next step. Then, ACT on the next step after that step.

You will be so busy performing the ACTIONS that you will forget about the top of the mountain. Someday you will wonder why you are in the clouds and looking back, you will realize that by ACTING on the little steps you have conquered the mountain.

There are just a couple more exercises left. Now that we have reached this stage of the journey, let me tell you a little bit about BRAVO Motivation™.

BRAVO stands for

Believe
Recognize
Act
Visualize
Obtain

I will discuss Bravo Motivation™ in detail in a later chapter.

In the meantime, let us talk about what is the best time to ACT. When you think about the actions you need to take in order to actualize your dream life, it is natural to feel that the timing may not be quite right. For example,

- The stock market is down and your portfolio is not quite where you want it to be.
- The housing market is stagnant.
- You are secure in your current place in life and do not want to take on added risk.
- The timing just does not feel right.

I have realized in my life that the timing is never right. There is always some reason why I could not ACT now. I know that if I look for reasons not to ACT, I will find many.

However, I have also RECOGNIZED the importance of acting now. I use the Bravo Motivation™ exercises on myself, whenever I feel unsure or hesitant about something. No matter what stage of life or what the problem I am facing. I perform the Bravo Motivation™ exercises and then ask myself the question. "If not now, when?"

There is only one reason to ACT now. The reason is that if you do not take ACT and take the first step, you will never begin the journey to self-realization. You will not be able to achieve that dream life until you ACT and ACT now.

I urge you to ask yourself, "If not now, when?"

IF NOT NOW, WHEN?

I am sure you have heard the saying there is no time like the present.

As I mentioned before, Once I have RECOGNIZED what is holding me back and identified how I need to ACT, I have trained my mind to ask the question, If not now, when?

Don't get me wrong, I am not asking you to live life with reckless abandon. I am not asking you to do anything reckless at all. In fact, I am all for being careful and safe.

However, I want you to realize that you can be careful and safe while taking steps and ACTING towards your goals. Look at the whole picture and find creative ways to take the steps that you need.

Look back at your list. Let us assume one of the things on there was to obtain some certification or qualification. Here is a creative way to ACT now. You do not have to quit your job, lose your income and start/restart school full-time. Instead, look for an evening or weekend program that will help you progress towards your goal. Yes, it will take longer. However, you will be making progress towards your goal and this in itself will create a joyous anticipation and urge to do something more.

Some of you are probably saying, "That is an easy example."

So let me deal with another one. You want to move into a smaller house after selling your current house, so you can reduce your monthly mortgage payment. Here are a few things you can do. How about staring to clean up your house and paint it, a wall at a time. Fix that broken hinge that you know the realtor will want you to fix prior to listing the house. Spruce up the yard. Trim back the over grown bushes and pull out he weeds.

Still think that was an easy example. How about something harder? You want to build up X dollars in your savings account before you venture out on that dream world-travel trip. OK, how about creating a budget and identifying what it is that you can do without. Maybe you do not need to eat out twice a week. Maybe you can live with basic cable instead of premium cable.

I hear what some of you are saying, "all right Atul, you keep picking easy examples. What if I want to find a new job in a new city?"

Let us see, maybe you can dust off your resume and format in a manner that is consistent with the new job you want. Post your resume on job-sites and search job-sites for jobs in the target city. Yes, these are all tiny steps, and by themselves, they do not mean much. However, each step you take brings you closer to your goal. It also fills you with anticipation. No! This is not the anxious nervous anticipation. This is a joyous anticipation, almost as if you know you are going to bump into something wonderful that is around the next corner.

I can still see sceptics out there. I hear you saying, "Atul these are all external things. What if I wanted to lose weight? Surely, that is hard."

Actually, I never said change is easy.

I already hear the sceptics saying, "Ah ha! I told you so."

You are right. I agree with you. It is not easy to do it all at once. However, try to break it down into manageable ACTIONS. Maybe you can research weight loss programs. Create a meal plan to lessen your calories. Maybe your problem is clinical. Consult a medical professional. These are all tiny steps that you can ACT on now.

Still not convinced? How about if your dream is to become a US senator? You could start by looking into the local city or county elections. That is a first step. If you already hold a position on the local city or county board, maybe you want to look into the state elections. These are all small steps. Nevertheless, each of them will bring you one-step closer to your ultimate dream.

Remember, you may not be able to leap over mountains in one single leap. Well maybe you can, but I cannot. However, if we ACT on one-step at a time and keep ACTING on the next step, you will eventually reach the top and be able to cross over to the other side

After the Rat Race

As I mentioned in the previous chapter, Patricia's words and another incident convinced me to change my lifestyle.

Here is the first incident. I am a type 'A' personality. I know I have said that before. In addition, at that time in my life, I was very impatient and used to get easily frustrated. The most common cause of my frustration was the traffic in the Washington, DC metro area.

All it took was someone to cut me off in traffic or take the parking spot that I was waiting to take. This was enough to ruin my entire day. Here is how it usually happened. Some inconsiderate jerk that is clearly in the wrong would cut me off.

Guess what happened next. Typically, some horn honking, some gesturing and more often than not some finger communication. After which I went my own way all frustrated, agitated and angry, muttering under my breath, thinking of all the things that I would have done to that person if only I had the time...

I carried this frustration with me all day and let it affect my mood and attitude. As a result, I was walking around with a bad attitude for the entire day. Furthermore, I projected this attitude on almost everyone with whom I came in contact.

However, that was not all. Things at work frustrated me also. While running the corporate rat race, I had become one of those people who got frustrated at the drop of a hat. The incident described below, made me reevaluate my thoughts and feelings when confronted with frustrating situations.

I was waiting in a parking lot in near the Rappahannock Complex in northern Virginia. I was driving a large Chevy Tahoe sport utility vehicle (SUV) at the time. Now, anyone that has ever driven or seen one of these behemoths knows that it is not easy to park them in just any parking space. They usually do not fit in the compact car spaces. I typically tried to look for parking spaces where other SUVs have parked, knowing that if that SUV fit, so will mine.

So when I saw another SUV starting to back out from a parking space. I put on my blinker and waited for him to back out. I also saw a small blue compact cruising around looking for a parking space. The SUV backed out of the parking space and since he was as large as I was, he blocked me for just a moment. In that instant, the small blue compact pulled in to the parking space for which I was waiting.

Now there could be absolutely no doubt in any reasonable person's mind that I was waiting for that parking space. I know that the person in the blue compact saw me and knew I was waiting for that parking space. He just happened to be one of those inconsiderate jerks I spoke about earlier.

I was enraged, I got ready to lean on my horn and was prepared to get out of the vehicle and duke it out if I had to. At that moment, out of the corner of my eye, I caught sight of an eagle (the Rappahannock Complex is a next to a bald eagle refuge) being chased by a few smaller birds. Crows or ravens I thought instinctively.

All thoughts of the blue compact vanished from my mind and I flashed back to my childhood. I recalled a conversation that I had with my father.

I was six or seven years old. We were traveling around the Isle of Skye in Scotland, on one of our many trips. My Dad pointed out a golden eagle that was being harassed several highland crows.

My father said; "Atul always watch the eagle and how he reacts when he is harassed by crows."

"Dad, he is flying away. He is a lot bigger why does he not fight and crush the crows?" was my childlike response.

My father continued, "Sure he can fight but why would he. Watch as he spreads his eight feet wide wing span and catches a thermal"

"Watch him rise ever so slowly and ever so majestically," dad said.

"Do you know that some eagles have been seen floating at eighteen thousand feet. That's the altitude where big passenger jets fly."

My father continued, "You know a crow has to flap his wings many times to just try and keep up with the eagle."

"What happens then," I said. "What happens when he catches the thermal and rises?"

"Simple" dad said, "The crow cannot fly at that altitude, if he tries, he will most probably die."

"Thus, when the eagle catches a thermal and rises, the crow can no longer harass the eagle," my father concluded.

How simple the logic behind this and how effective. I decided immediately that in my situation with the blue compact, I should be like the eagle and rise above the situation. I took a deep breath; thought about the eagle and said to myself I can rise above this situation. I am not going to let the crow in the blue compact harass me for any longer than it takes me to catch that proverbial mental thermal and rise above.

Guess what, it worked. I suddenly felt much better. I was not frustrated and I had a great meeting with the client that I was visiting. The client actually commented on my exuberance and positive attitude, especially after driving through the Washington, DC beltway traffic.

"Thank you dad." was all I could say under my breath. The memory of this incident did a lot more for me than just teach me to effectively deal with people who cut me off in traffic and/or take my parking space.

Do not get me wrong. I am not trying to say that I do not get frustrated or angry. I am not a saint, I am a red-blooded human and do feel emotions including anger and frustration. I just found a way to deal with my negative emotions in a very positive manner. By following this philosophy, I am only angry or frustrated for as long as it takes me to picture the eagle and catch my mental thermal.

I also realized another thing. By letting someone get me all angry and frustrated, I effectively gave him or her control over my emotions and me. Without exchanging a word, I have surrendered to them.

Almost akin to saying, "yes you have the power. One action by you and you can take away my good mood and optimism. You can take away my positive attitude. You can take away my peace of mind. Finally, you can ruin my entire day."

No! I will not let anyone have control over my peace of mind any more.

Now I say to myself, "I am in complete control of my mind, my feelings, and my emotions. Only I have the power to decide how I am going to feel today."

Once I started thinking this way, it was almost as if a big heavy burden was lifted off my shoulders. I began to feel as if I could accomplish anything. I had the ability to shake negative emotions as soon as they began to affect me.

Thanks again dad. You are so right. The eagle does not have to turn around and fight with the crows. He just needs to spread his wings and rise above it all.

This incident was punctuated a few weeks later with my wife's words that snapped me back to reality. When I told her about the life insurance, she said; "If I only wanted money, I could have married someone a lot richer that you."

"I want someone that would spend their life with me."

"I want someone I can grow old with."

"What good is the money to me if you are dead?"

With those words and that conversation, she reminded me about what was important. She told me in very matter of fact manner that she would prefer living in a smaller house with lesser things just as long as we were able to spend more time with each other.

"Money is not important, power is not important, position is not important, but love surely is." She said.

At that very moment, I had an epiphany. I flashed back again to an incident that took place when I was backpacking around the world.

I was about eighteen and almost finished with my yearlong travel the world quest that I mentioned in an earlier chapter. I spent several months in Mauritius after trekking through Central Africa. I will talk about my trek through Africa some other time, in some other book. Right now, I want to elaborate on one particular experience in Mauritius.

Mauritius is a beautiful island nation in the Indian Ocean approximately one thousand three hundred nautical miles off the South East Coast of Africa. The island, which is of volcanic origin, covers an area of approximately seven hundred twenty square miles. Coral reefs surround most of the coast except the south.

The waters are blue and clear like a swimming pool.

The average high is 80° F and the average low is 65° F. There are really only two seasons. It is hot and rainy from November to April and it is warm, and dry from May to October. English is the official language. However, most folks are multi-lingual and speak English and French or English and Creole.

Anyway, I am not going to get too lost in the beauty of Mauritius and its people. Let us just say that it is another Hawaii without all the commercialization. At least that is the way it was when I went there many decades ago.

The point of bringing up Mauritius was to describe a unique experience that I had when I was visiting the island. Since I spent several months there, I became a regular at the Grand Baie beachfront. The locals were all very friendly. However, I started hanging around one particular group of locals, about the same age group as me, who were also regulars at the beach. After the first week or so, they began including me in their conversations and their partying.

One particular evening, someone the group brought up the topic of occupations and aspirations. We soon began talking about what we all did and what we wanted to do. Some people were sugar cane harvesters by profession and worked three days a week. Others were fishermen. The occupations were as diverse as the people were.

When I was asked what I planned to do when I got back home, I had my answer ready. I told them that I was planning to go to college, study engineering, and get a master's degree and so on...

After answering, I asked one person in particular what she did for a living. She was a lovely Creole woman named Chantal. I had taken a liking to her over the past few weeks and she had reciprocated. However, that is another story altogether.

Chantal told me that she owned a small glass bottom boat. Her father had left her the boat as a means to make a living. I had seen several of these boats in the makeshift marina. Tourists hired these boats to get rides up to the coral reefs and looked at the rich and colorful marine life in Mauritius through the glass bottom.

She also told me that she only ran the boat about two or three days a week sometimes less. It is no wonder that she was on the beach all the time. Not that I was complaining, I actually liked seeing her there.

My instinctive reaction to this was "OK Chantal, you already own the boat, why don't you run it every day?"

She said, "What happens if I run the boat every day?"

I replied, "You will make a lot of profit and then you can buy another boat and hire someone to run it,"

"Now you will have two boats and the profits will grow much faster." I continued. "With that profit you can buy another boat and if you keep doing this, soon you will have a fleet of boats and be rich."

"Let's say that I do what you are telling me and get rich, then what should I do?" Chantal queried.

"That is easy," I said, "You can do anything your heart desires."

"You can buy a big house, sell your business, bank the money and then relax and spend your time anyway you like, without any worries what so ever."

"Isn't that exactly what I am doing now?" she asked pragmatically.

I was flabbergasted. Here I had this entire logical argument on why she should work hard and earn more money and…

Her simple response just took the wind out of my sails. At that moment in time, I swore to myself that I would be like Chantal and the other people in that group I met in Mauritius. I was not going to waste my life in the corporate world blah blah blah.

I was going to complete my degree so that I had something to fall back on. Then I was going to enjoy life just like Chantal and the others on that beach in Mauritius. I thought then that I had my life all figured out. I never for a moment thought that I would become addicted to the corporate rat race.

Therefore, when I left Mauritius, I planned my life out on the plane ride to America, the last stop on my world tour. I planned to go back to London, complete just enough college to earn a degree and then head for the nearest island.

Life was going to be fun, fun and more fun. When I landed in the US on the last leg of my travel the world quest, I took one look at New York and Washington, DC and lost more than two decades of my life in the blink of an eye.

However, the Mauritius incident mentioned above was more than two decades prior to when Patricia had her "what is really important" conversation with me.

Alas! Where did those two decades go?

Over the period of those two decades, I had worked hard, studied a lot, got my bachelor's degree, studied further, and even completed my PhD. I had held many big titles at prestigious firms including senior vice president of operations. However, had I really accomplished anything of significance in those two decades?

What would have happened if I had suffered from a stroke that day prior to getting to the doctor's office? What would my epitaph say?

"Here lies a man who slaved for Corporate America till the day he died. In the process he ignored his family, his friends and everyone else who loved him for what he was inside."

Not a very good sounding epitaph is it.

Conversely, what if I had done what I had initially planned and after completing my degree gone back to Mauritius or even London. Where would I be now?

I honestly do not know the answer to that question.

I now believe that we all have a higher purpose in life. We are not placed on this earth to work and work until we can work no more.

I remember a movie that said something to the effect, "you make more money so that you can invest it and make even more money and the one that has the most when he dies wins."

Is this really what life is all about? For a little over two decades, that is exactly what life was all about for me. Moreover, for many people this still is a way of life.

So where do I go from here. I can do nothing to change the past. The past is done and gone. I have lost two decades of my life and no amount of lamenting, guilt or pining is going to bring those years back. However, I have the ability to control what I do in the present and in the future.

I decided instead to concentrate on what I could do going forward. I quit my job almost immediately. My wife and I started a small limited liability company (LLC). Our company started with two employees (Patricia and Atul). For as long as it survives, it will always have the same two employees. We do not intend to upsize, right size, IPO, M&A or any of those other acronyms. We just want to make enough money to support the necessities of our life. Together we are finally doing the very thing she had been urging me to do for years and we are now happy.

However, it was not all roses in the beginning. There is no feeling as scary as leaving something that has become your second nature for a major part of your life. At first, I was unsure, I was afraid and I lacked the confidence. Do not get me wrong, I never doubted my skills or my ability. However, not having corporate America felt just as if I was a tortoise that had lost its shell. I felt naked and vulnerable.

I have often heard the cliché that behind every successful man is a woman. I do not know about the rest of the world. I can only speak for myself. I would not have made it without the constant encouragement and support that Patricia offers me on a daily basis.

Did I make as much money as I did when I was working within the confines of corporate America? The answer is a resounding no. Did we have to give up the three thousand square foot four bedroom three and half bathroom house? You betcha!

However, not all the money in the world can buy what matters most. My family and friends enjoy being around me. What matters most to me is that Patricia is finally happy. I am able to give her exactly what she needed and it does not cost me any money.

Patricia now has someone to spend quality time with her and grow old with her.

The good old boy from Romford, the one that had kissed the Blarney Stone one too many a time was back, or so I thought.

I wish I could say that I had learned my lesson completely. However, it is not easy to walk away from addiction of any kind. Sure, I had made some major changes. I will not bore you with the details. They were uneventful, as I had very diligently done the RECOGNIZE-ACT exercises as described earlier. I took step after little step and reached what I thought was the top of the mountain.

Unfortunately, I had not learned the lesson of "VISUALIZE" just yet. Consequently, I stopped short of where I wanted to be, always assuming that I had achieved my goal.

Here are some of the changes I achieved:

- I relocated to a place with a less expensive cost of living
- I left Corporate America and started my own business
- I sold my big house and moved to a smaller house with a much smaller mortgage

Here is the primary thing I did not change.

- I did not change my mind set. I did not change my paradigm.

This would prove to be my downfall and lead me into the wakeup call that I do not wish on anyone in this world. However, before I take you down that path; it is time again for me to invite you to the next exercise…

Visualize

You may be wondering why you should VISUALIZE?

I can tell you from personal experience. Visualization is a very powerful tool. Simply put, visualization works because our subconscious brain cannot tell the difference between real and imagined. I know there is a lot of research available on the subject so, I am not going to delve into technical details of how visualization works in this book.

If you would like to find out more, I recommend that you perform internet searches on key words such as "Law of Attraction," "Vision Boards," "Creative Visualization," etc. You will find that professional athletes often use these techniques.

In addition, I would be lying if I told you that I could teach you how exactly to visualize or what specific visualization technique will work for you.

How it works is that I can merely teach you the concepts of visualization. Then, you have to figure out how to make visualization work for you.

After leaving northern Virginia, Patricia and I lived about eight miles from the Virginia Beach oceanfront for several years. Once the kids were grown up and gone, we wanted to move to a Condo at the Virginia Beach Oceanfront. In addition, we only wanted to move to one of two high-rise Condo buildings (located on Atlantic Avenue between 38th and 40th street). Let me first tell you what we did and then I'll tell you why.

- We went on Google Earth and printed out an image of the area of interest, making sure the image clearly depicted the two high-rise Condo buildings that we liked.

- We made many copies of this image and pasted it in every area of the house where we were certain to see it many times during the day.

- We made sure that at least one image was in an area that we saw first thing in the morning and last thing at night. The areas where we posted images are listed below.

  » The bathroom mirror
  » Inside my closet

- » The mirror on Patricia's dresser
- » In my office on the wall just above the computer monitor
- » Inside the medicine cabinet

- Then here is what we did, every time we saw the image, we would pause for ten seconds and visualize what it would feel like to live in that area.

- Whenever we visited the oceanfront, we would always find parking on or around 40th street and sit on the beach in the vicinity, just as if we would do if we lived in one of those two high-rise Condo buildings.

Nothing happened for almost three years. Then suddenly, out of the blue, a Condo became available at one of those buildings and we were able to buy it at a very reasonable price.

We are now living in our dream Condo on 39th and Atlantic. When we go to the beach, we just walk across the street to the same spot where we went for the past three years. One big difference, we do have to find parking on 40th street, because our cars are in the Condo's parking lot.

Let me break down the visualization that Patricia and I did to get the Condo we wanted.

Step 1: We found images of what we wanted.

Step 2: We posted images that would remind us of where we wanted to live.

This is the easy part. However, knowing that we would be there someday in the future was not enough. You see, the subconscious mind has a very specific connotation attached to what is in the future versus what is in the present. Therefore, we had to teach our subconscious brain to believe that this was happening in the present.

Step 3: Every time we passed any one of the images, we would pause for ten seconds, close our eyes feel like we lived in that area. We imagined what the ocean would sound like; we imagined sitting on the balcony and feeling the ocean breeze, etc.

Step 4: In order to convince our subconscious brain further, we would only sit on the beach in the exact area where we would be if we lived one of those two high-rise Condo buildings. Let me tell you that this was not easy as the closest public parking lot was on 31st street. Therefore, we would have to go earlier in the day and find on-street metered parking around 40th street. Moreover, the closest public restrooms are on 32nd street. It was a royal pain in the BLEEP, but we did it for three years.

People that I coach often ask me, "Do I really have to do this visualization thing?"

I always answer them with this question, "How much do you want to actualize your dream life?"

Step 5: Keep doing steps 3 and 4 with unwavering faith and determination.

Simple note: You have to believe with all your being that you have already achieved your dream and keep at it until the dream becomes reality.

The concept of visualization is very simple yet it is one of the hardest steps in Bravo Motivation™.

We are almost done with the exercises, just a little more.

However, before we discuss the last and final step, let me take you back to my journey.

Awakening and the Present

Earlier, I mentioned that I had not learned my lesson completely. Here is what I mean. I had completed and followed on the RECOGNIZE and ACT exercise. However, I had not performed the VISUALIZE portion of BRAVO Motivation™. Consequently, I stopped short of where I wanted to be. However, I assumed all along that I had achieved my goal.

While I had made many changes, the primary thing I did not change was my mindset and my paradigm. Let me tell you what happened.

I started my own business in 2004. This was a major step towards actualizing my dream life and I achieved success. However, not having visualized, I started falling back on old patterns. Slowly but surely, I started working more and more. I started adding unnecessary pressure on myself. Once again, the Type "A" Atul came to the forefront and I lost sight of what was really important in my life.

The wakeup call came silently and unexpectedly. I was driving home one Thursday in April 2009 when I felt a sharp pain in my stomach. My thoughts immediately turned to lunch and I said to myself, "I wish I had not eaten that second chicken kabob."

I took several deep breaths and continued driving while I felt severe heartburn coming on. At least that is what I thought it was at that time.

I continued taking deep breaths as I was driving, and the pain subsided. I swore to myself that I would lay off the greasy food. This promise usually works until the next time I see/smell the temptation. Well, I am human after all. I still felt some discomfort that I attributed to heartburn. I took an antacid pill and did my best to put it out of my mind.

I got home safely and spent a quiet evening with Patricia. We normally try to go out to dinner when I get back home on Thursdays. However, that night I informed Patricia that I was feeling run down and tired from a busy workweek so we stayed at home had an early dinner and I went to bed.

My typical Friday morning routine was to drink tea, check email and then commence my work out. On Friday April 10, I woke up at my normal time between

5:00 and 5:30 a.m. and I started brewing a cup of tea and fired up my laptop.

More often than not, something would show up in email and throw my entire day's plans out the window. I noticed an email that morning which required my immediate attention. Moreover, that email irritated me and got my dander up, so to speak. I typed up a response and as I hit <SEND>, I felt a sledge hammer-like blow in my chest.

I started feeling dizzy. I was not quite sure what was happening. I made my way up the stairs and woke my wife up. I told her I was feeling unwell and that I probably needed to lie down for a few minutes and maybe I would feel better.

My wife asked me if I was feeling hot. "No," I replied. "Actually I am feeling a little chilly."

"That's very odd," she said. "You are covered in sweat."

No sooner had I lain down than I felt an overwhelming sense of nausea and I began dry heaving. Patricia suggested that we call 9–1–1 for an ambulance. Of course, that would have been the sensible thing to do. However, I am a man and a hardheaded one at that. I insisted on her driving me.

I will not elaborate this story here as I have chronicled it in great detail in my book "Remember Thou Art Mortal."

Here is the short version. I had suffered a massive heart attack. I learned later from my cardiologist that less than 5% of people come back after suffering this type of heart attack.

It took me two more years to come to my senses. Patricia stood by me every step of the way. I finally completed the VISUALIZATION exercise. I took the time and VISUALIZED my life the way I wanted it to be. I will not reiterate the visualization process here, instead let me tell you what I have achieved.

I can honestly say one thing. I now live life to the fullest and enjoy every minute. I am personally happier and really look forward to each day. I look forward to the sun, the breeze, the rain, the water, the birds and the flowers. Anything and everything that nature has to offer. I look forward to seeing my wife's beautiful face first thing when I wake up and last thing before I go to bed. Everything in life is a miracle. Often, when people ask me how I am doing, I respond by saying, "Any day I wake up and see sky and not roots is a wonderful day."

I cannot bring back those twenty-five years, twenty spent in corporate rate race and five spent in the race after the rat race. However, I know what I can do. I can live the next few decades in the manner in which I should have done in the first place.

Leaving a way of life that I had grown accustomed to

over a period of two and half decades is not easy. I still feel the pangs of longing tugging at me from time to time. Just like a recovering addict feels the need for that one last fix.

Nowadays, I only work about twenty or thirty hours every week. A rough week is forty hours. The rest of my time, I spend with my family and those that mean the most to me. Those that love me for who I really am and not for what I can accomplish.

I have slowed down my consulting practice to a bare minimum. After 29 years in the corporate world, I decided to devote the rest of my life to coaching and helping others achieve their full potential through targeted motivation programs.

I do this through simple, realistic tools and techniques that are easy to apply in your life. No! These are not cookie-cutter tools, this is a customized individual plan tailored to your specific needs. I help people achieve clarity and focus. I help people set priorities that leverage their strengths and passion. My approach helps people achieve their full potential while maintaining a healthy work-life balance and fulfillment in all aspects of life.

Coaching is a very fulfilling profession. I truly believe that I make a difference in people's life by essentially motivating them to realize their full potential.

I no longer look at life as a distraction from work. Rather, I look at work as a distraction from life. Don't get me wrong. I realize that we all need to work. We all need money to pay the mortgage, the bills, etc. However, amongst all this we need to remember that we work so that we may live and not the other way around.

I am confident that I am past the hump. However, my arrogance has not returned. The pills that I take to regulate my heart rate are a constant reminder. In addition, I have to live carefully on blood thinners for the rest of my life. I have to be careful about my diet and my lifestyle. I have to continue to hope that the stents will last their entire theoretical 30-year life span and maybe some more.

I am thankful to be alive. I am thankful that I am able to enjoy life with my lovely wife. I am proud to see my son and daughter grow up and become a young man and woman respectively. Most importantly, I am overjoyed to enjoy my grandkids and see them grow from infants to toddlers. I continue to hope that if I keep doing everything right, I will be around to see them grow up into young adults as well.

Whenever I have the opportunity to do something new and positive or whenever I am stuck, I perform the Bravo Motivation™ exercise. I identify my ACTIONS and ask myself. "If not now, when?"

Obtain

Obtain. What do you think this means?

Well the dictionary defines obtain as follows: to gain or attain usually by planned action or effort.

Well, you RECOGNIZED, ACTED and VISUALIZED so now it is time to enjoy what you have earned because of your actions and efforts.

An important part of OBTAINING is to accept, enjoy and to be in a constant state of thankfulness, gratitude and grace.

Several clients ask me why they need to accept and enjoy once they have achieved something.

It is quite simple really and extremely critical. The subconscious mind is always trying to make real or create the primary feeling that you visualize.

If after OBTAINING, if you do not maintain an attitude of thankfulness and grace, you will fall back into old thoughts and patterns.

As a result, your subconscious mind will make this a reality and take you right back to where you started.

It is important to have gratitude and enjoyment at all times. This will being more gratitude and enjoyment.

Just remember, the primary premise of OBTAIN is to maintain and attitude of thankfulness and grace.

It also includes being able to take a breather to accept, enjoy what you have achieved. Remember success is a journey. When you reach a certain step in the journey, savor it, enjoy it and relish the feeling before commencing on the next step.

Yes, you have momentum and your momentum will want you to keep pushing forward. However, without taking the time to enjoy and live your accomplishments, you will create your own self-perpetuating hamster wheel.

Moreover, by taking the time to enjoy and live out your accomplishment, you will get a chance to think and plan your next step. Remember that your next step may change based on what you have achieved thus far.

This might be a good point to apply the BRAVO Motivation™ exercise once again. Enough said.

Bravo Motivation™

BRAVO stands for

Believe
Recognize
Act
Visualize
Obtain

BELIEVE: This is the process of truly acknowledg-ing and accepting your powers and skills. It involves knowing at a fundamental level with you whole being that you are capable of achieving whatever goals and objectives you set for yourself.

RECOGNIZE: This is the process of being brutally honest with yourself and identifying the following:

1. What it is that you would really like to do or be

2. What are the obstacles that may keep you from achieving your dream
3. What skills, knowledge and capabilities you have acquired in your life thus far.

ACT: You identify positive actions and/or steps necessary to overcome the obstacles during this process. Then you execute these steps and make progress towards achieving your dream.

VISUALIZE: This is the process of convincing your subconscious mind that you are already living your dream. This process programs the subconscious mind to accept the new reality as already existent.

OBTAIN: This is the process of accepting and enjoying what you have earned because of your actions and efforts.

You have had a glimpse of a very powerful tool for self-motivation that can help you achieve anything and everything you desire and lead you to live the actualized and joyous life that you deserve.

It is now up to you to put this into practice and create your own reality. I hope you have fun.

BRAVO
BRAVO
BRAVO

Don't just sit there, get up. Complete the exercise.

Make the lists. If you already made the list, take the first step that you identified and the next one after that. ACT. ACT now.

IF NOT NOW, WHEN?
IF NOT NOW, WHEN?

Thank you for reading my book.
http://www.bravomotivation.com/

Other Books by the Author

- **Uchil, A.** "Remember Thou Art Mortal: The Chronicles of a Mending Heart" (2012) Outskirts Press, Inc. **ISBN:** 978-1478715887

"Remember Thou Art Mortal" received the Readers Views Reviewers Choice Literary Award.

Every event in life – good or not – changes the course of our lives in some way. For Atul Uchil it was as big an event in life as one could experience without ending life itself: a heart attack. Some 600,000 Americans experience a heart attack each year, but not everyone who survives uses the experience to change their lives and the lives of others. Dr. Uchil tackles the struggles to fight back from a heart attack with Remember Thou Art Mortal: The Chronicles of a Mending Heart. Dr. Uchil tells a very personal account of a post-heart-attack life in a surprisingly warm and candid book that also happens to be preciously informative. Far from a dry, medical tome, Remember Thou Art Mortal intersperses Dr. Uchil's narrative with useful breakdowns of medical terminology, his first-person description of heart attack symptoms, and advice on dietary changes that could help prevent heart attack and much more..

- **Uchil, A.** "Goals-Based Strategic Planning: A No-Nonsense Practical Guide To Strategy" (2009) Outskirts Press, Inc. **ISBN:** 978-1432723309

The strategic planning process is fairly simple and straightforward. The difficult part is that strategic planning is extremely subjective. Understanding the terms and having a good grasp of what they represent is critical. In order to generate a good strategic plan and the associated work products, it is not sufficient to know the textbook definition of the terms. It is vital to understand the underlying purpose and intent of the work product represented by each term.

There are a myriad of models and approaches used in strategic planning. Goals-based strategic planning is the most prevalent method. Therefore, the information in this book is discussed in reference to goals-based strategic planning.

- **Uchil, A**. "Relationship Selling: The Fine Art OF Consultative Sales" (2007) Outskirts Press, Inc. **ISBN:** 978-1432715007

  Everyone has heard the following: People like to buy - People hate being sold or being forced to buy - People buy from people that they like and trust.

  Therefore, it stands to reason that if you are the person your clients trust they will buy from you without you having to sell them anything. How then do you become the trusted advisor to your clients? How do you establish and maintain long-term relationships? This book reveals the best kept secrets of successful relationship selling and is a must-read for every consultant and sales professional.

- **Uchil, A**. "The Corporate America Survival Handbook: A Cornucopia of Essential Information" (2005) Outskirts Press, Inc. **ISBN:** 978-1598000942

  THE CORPORATE AMERICA SURVIVAL HANDBOOK is deliberately narrated in a format that lets the readers go to whatever section they need and read it independently of other sections.

  This book is a powerful tool, providing information on a wide variety of topics, including security clearances, the job market, resume writing, patents, trademarks and much more.

This book does not contain any magical formula for success - it is mostly common sense. However, this book gives the reader many invaluable insights into Corporate America that most people do not know.

As the saying goes, "Common sense in an uncommon degree is what the world calls wisdom."

- **Uchil, A**. "Consulting: A Job Or A Lifestyle." (2005) Outskirts Press, Inc. **ISBN:** 978-1598000640

  CONSULTING: A JOB OR A LIFESTYLE contains comprehensive research into the life of persons that choose consulting as a career. It details the pros and cons including the lifestyle sacrifices that are an integral part of consulting.

- **Uchil, A**. "I Opted Out: The Chronicles Of A Rat Race Junkie." (2005) Outskirts Press, Inc. **ISBN:** 978-1598000713

  I OPTED OUT, narrated in the form of a pseudo-autobiography, takes a poignant and satirical look at the impact of the corporate rat race on the personal life of an individual that is addicted to his work.

  Today's society often parades the term 'workaholic' as a catch phrase or a badge of honor. Few recognize that addiction to work can be as dangerous as addiction to drugs or alcohol. The

author presents this material in a humorous manner, where possible, to lighten the burden of reading, while taking care not to let humor dilute the
gravity of the message.

CPSIA information can be obtained at www.ICGtesting.com
Printed in the USA
BVOW04s1249020115

381636BV00006B/18/P